5S for Operators

5 Pillars of the Visual Workplace

5S for Operators

5 Pillars of the Visual Workplace

Created by
The Productivity Press
Development Team

Based on
5 Pillars of the Visual Workplace:
The Sourcebook for 5S Implementation
by Hiroyuki Hirano

Instructional Design
by Melanie Rubin

Productivity Press

New York

Adapted from Hiroyuki Hirano, *5 Pillars of the Visual Workplace: The Sourcebook for 5S Implementation*, English edition © 1995 by Productivity Press (based on *5S shido manyuaru*, © 1990 by Nikkan Kogyo Shimbun, Ltd., Tokyo, Japan).

Productivity Press
444 Park Avenue South, 7th floor
New York, NY 10016
United States of America
Telephone: 212-686-5900
Telefax: 212-686-5411
E-mail: info@productivitypress.com

Book and cover design by William Stanton

Cover illustration by Gary Ragaglia

Graphics by Productivity Press (India) Private Ltd., Rohani Design, and Matthew C. DeMaio

Page composition by Matthew C. DeMaio

Printed and bound by Malloy Lithographing, Inc. in the United States of America

Library of Congress Cataloging-in-Publication Data

5S for operators : 5 pillars of the visual workplace / created by the Productivity Press
    Development Team : instructional design by Melanie Rubin.
        p.   cm.
    Based on: 5 pillars of the visual workplace / Hiroyuki Hirano. 1995.
    Includes bibliographical references (p.   )
    ISBN: 1-56327-123-0 (Paperback)
    1. Factory management.   2. Office management.   I. Hirano, Hiroyuki. 5 pillars
of the visual workplace.   II. Productivity Press Development Team.

TS155.   1996
658.5–dc20   95-53802
                                                                              CIP

15 14 13   7 8 9 10

Contents

3. The First Pillar: Sort

4. The Second Pillar: Set in Order

5. The Third Pillar: Shine

6. The Fourth Pillar: Standardize

7. The Fifth Pillar: Sustain

8. Reflections and Conclusions

Publisher's Message

This book is intended to give you powerful knowledge that you can use to make your workplace cleaner and safer and your job simpler and more satisfying. It's about how to create a workplace that is clearly organized, free of clutter, arranged so you can find things, and sparkling clean—a place where anyone would be proud to work. What you will learn about here is often called the "5S method," a reference to five words for the basic elements of this system: Sort, Set in Order, Shine, Standardize and Sustain.* These activities are truly 5 pillars of an effective workplace. (This book will use 5S and five pillars as interchangeable terms.)

The 5S approach is simple and universal. It works in companies all over the world. 5S activities provide essential support for successful implementation of other important manufacturing improvements in your company, such as shorter equipment changeovers, just-in-time inventory systems, total quality management, and total productive maintenance.

This book was developed from concepts in a longer book, *5 Pillars of the Visual Workplace*, which was written for managers. When you get right down to it, though, you—the frontline production and assembly associates—are the people who will be most involved in implementing the 5S approach—and also the ones who will benefit the most from it. We have developed this book specifically to give you the 5S basics in a straightforward format we think you will find interesting and accessible.

5S for Operators presents an overview of the five pillars, then devotes a separate chapter to each one. The first chapter of the book is like an "owner's manual" that tells you how to get the most out of your reading by using margin assists, summaries, and other features to help you pull out what you need to know.

One of the most effective ways to use this book is to read and discuss it with other employees in group learning sessions. We have deliberately planned the book so that it can be used this way, with chunks of information that can be covered in a series of short sessions. Each chapter includes reflection questions to stimulate group discussion. A Learning Package is also available, which includes a leader's guide, overhead transparencies to summarize major points, and color slides showing case examples of 5S activities implementation.

We hope this book will show you how easy it is to implement 5S and how you can apply it to make your workplace a better place to spend your time.

Acknowledgments

Productivity would like first to acknowledge Hiroyuki Hirano for writing 5 *Pillars of the Visual Workplace*, the book upon which *5S for Operators* is based. Mr. Hirano has formulated the concepts and tools of the 5S system in a way that makes them readily accessible to the management of manufacturing companies throughout the English-speaking world.

Many people contributed to the design and editing of this text and in some cases to the further development of the content. We would like to express heartfelt thanks to Dee Tadlock of Read Right Systems for her extensive instructional design input and review throughout this project. Dr. Tadlock's expertise in text analysis and workforce reading requirements were a critical influence in shaping the design of this book.

The form and content of this book were also heavily influenced by input from Productivity customers. Thanks are due to the participants in two Productivity focus groups conducted in September, 1995: Jerry Dowd, Lee Garrett, Joe Jacobs, Henry Jedrzejek, Michael Keck, Ron Kraus, Jim Leflar, Ray Nutt, Randy Quick, Paul Rottenberg, and Michael Williams. Thanks also go to Productivity customers who reviewed the manuscript, including Lee Garrett, Joe Jacobs, Henry Jedrzejek, Michael Keck, Ron Kraus, Clyde Melton, Raymond Nutt, Mark O'Brien, Rick Pollett, Steven Pralley, Jaymie Randel, Paul Rottenberg, and Steve Warywoda.

Within Productivity, the development of this book has been a strong team effort. Melanie Rubin did a wonderful job of extracting the practical essence of the original book and developing an appropriate instructional design format, as well as planning additional materials to enhance the content. Steven Ott, Diane Asay, and Karen Jones played major roles in the product definition, development, and editorial stages. Tom Fabrizio gave instructional design input and advice. Mary Pat Crum, Tim Hickey, Carla Comarella and Patricia Slote of the sales and marketing team provided input to the product concept and design. Charles Skinner contributed a detailed content review. Bill Stanton created the design. Julie Zinkus proofread the manuscript and Susan Swanson managed the production.

Considerable thanks are also due Matthew C. DeMaio for his production work on this book under a challenging schedule. His design and typesetting were skilled and conscientious, and his illustrations added a welcome element of humor.

Finally, the staff at Productivity Press wishes to acknowledge the good work of the many people who are now in the process of implementing the 5S system in their own organizations. We welcome any feedback about this book, as well as input about how we can continue to serve you in your 5S implementation efforts.

Norman Bodek
Chairman, Productivity, Inc.

---

* The original 5S terms are five Japanese words beginning with "S." The first printings of this book used the following translations for these five terms:

Organization	(Sort)
Orderliness	(Set in Order)
Cleanliness	(Shine)
Standardized Cleanup	(Standardize)
Discipline	(Sustain)

We are now using the five "S" terms shown in the right column to help readers remember them more easily. These terms were developed by Productivity's Client Services Group to support 5S implementation in the workplace.

Chapter 1. Getting Started

CHAPTER OVERVIEW

Purpose of This Book

What the Book is Based On

Two Ways to Use This Book

How to Get the Most Out of Your Reading

- Becoming Familiar with This Book
- How to Read Each Chapter
- Explanation of Reading Strategy
- Using Margin Assists

Overview of the Contents

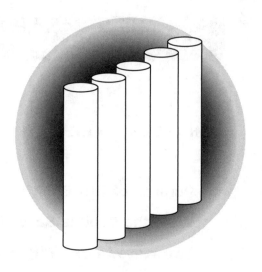

Purpose of This Book

5S for Operators was written to give you the information you need to participate in implementing the 5S method in your company. As you already know, you are a valued member of your company's team. Your knowledge, support, and participation are essential to the success of any major effort in your organization.

The paragraph you have just read explains the author's purpose in writing this book. It also explains why your company may wish you to read this book.

Key Point

But why are you reading this book? This question is even more important. *What you get out of this book largely depends on what you are trying to get out of it.*

You may be reading this book because your supervisor or manager has asked you to do so. Or, you may be reading it because you think it will provide information that will help you in your work. By the time you finish Chapter 2, you will have a better idea of how the information in this book can help you make your job more satisfying and more efficient. You will also have a sense of how the 5S activities will make your workplace a safer, cleaner, and more pleasant place to work.

Figure 1-1. The Book *5 Pillars of the Visual Workplace*

What This Book is Based On

This book is based on Hiroyuki Hirano's book, 5 Pillars of the Visual Workplace, also published by Productivity Press (see Figure 1-1). It presents the main concepts and tools of Mr. Hirano's book in a shortened and simplified format that requires less time and effort to read than the original book. The original book is useful as a cross-reference for more detailed information on many subjects, including topics related to the design of a 5S implementation program.

Two Ways to Use This Book

There are at least two ways to use this book (see Figure 1–1): 1) as the reading material for a learning group or study group process within your company and 2) for learning on your own. Productivity Press offers a Learning Package product that uses *5S for Operators* as the foundation reading material for a learning group. Your company may decide instead to design its own learning group process based on *5S for Operators*. Or, you may buy or be given this book to read on your own.

How to Get the Most Out of Your Reading

Becoming Familiar with This Book

How-to Steps

There are a few steps you can follow to make it easier to absorb the information in this book. We've included a suggested amount of time for each step.

1. Scan the Contents to see how this book is set up (1 minute).

2. Complete Chapter 1 for an overview of the book's contents (5 minutes).

3. Flip through the book to get a feel for its style, flow, and design. Notice how the chapters are structured and glance at the pictures (3 minutes).

4. Read parts of Chapter 8, "Reflections and Conclusions," to get a sense of the book's direction (2 minutes).

How to Read Each Chapter

How-to Steps

For each chapter in this book we suggest you follow these steps to get the most out of your reading.

1. Read the "Chapter Overview" on the first page (1 minute).

2. Flip through the chapter, looking at the way it is laid out. (1 minute).

3. Ask yourself, "Based on what I've seen in this chapter so far, what questions do I have about the material?" (1 minute).

4. Then read the chapter. How long this takes depends on what you already know about the content and what you are trying to get out of your reading. As you read:

   • Use the margin assists to help you follow the flow of information.

   • If the book is your own, highlight key information and answers to your questions about the material. If the book is not your own, take notes on a separate sheet of paper.

   • Answer the "Take Five" questions in the text. These will help you to absorb the information by reflecting on how you can implement it.

5. Finally, read the "Chapter Summary" in each chapter to confirm what you learned. If you don't remember something in the summary, find that section in the chapter and review it (3 minutes).

Explanation of Reading Strategy

These steps are based on two simple principles about the way your brain learns. First, as an analogy, it is difficult to build a house unless a framework is put in place. Similarly, it's difficult for your brain to absorb new information if it does not have a structure to place it in.

Key Point

By getting an overview of the contents and then flipping through the materials, you give your brain a framework for the new information in this book. Within each chapter, you repeat this process on a smaller scale, by reading the main points, summary, and headings first.

Key Point

Second, *it is a lot easier to learn if you take it a layer at a time, instead of trying to absorb all the information at once.* In terms of our house analogy, you can rarely paint a brand new wall with the first coat of paint. It is better to lay down a coat of primer, then one coat of finish paint, and later a final finish coat.

When people read a book, they usually think they should start with the first word and read straight through until the end. This is not usually the best way to learn from a book. The method we've described here is easier, more fun, and more effective.

Using Margin Assists

As you've noticed by now, this book uses margin assists to help you follow the information in each chapter. There are eight types of margin assists.

- Background Information — Sets the stage for what comes next
- Overview — Presents new information without the detail presented later
- Definition — Explains how the author uses key terms
- Key Point — Highlights important ideas to remember
- New Tool — Helps you apply what you have learned
- Example — Helps you understand the key points
- How-to Steps — Gives you a set of directions for using new tools
- Principle — Explains how things work in a variety of situations

Overview of the Contents

Chapter 1. Getting Started (pages 1-9)

This is the chapter you're reading now. It explains the purpose of this book and how it was written. Then it gives you tips for getting the most out of your reading. Finally, it gives you an overview of each chapter.

Chapter 2. Introduction and Overview (pages 11-27)

There are five pillars in Hiroyuki Hirano's Visual Workplace system (5S). Chapter 2 in 5S *for Operators* starts by defining the word "pillar" and explaining why these five pillars are needed in a company. It gives a short explanation of each of the five pillars. Then it describes some common types of resistance to implementing 5S activities. Finally, it reviews the benefits you and your company will experience when the 5S program is implemented.

Chapter 3. The First Pillar: Sort (pages 29-43)

Chapter 3 introduces and defines the first pillar, *Sort*. It explains why the first pillar is important, and describes problems that are avoided by implementing it. Then it explains the concepts, tools, and steps in the Red-Tagging Strategy, a technique used to implement the Sort pillar in any company.

Chapter 4. The Second Pillar: Set in Order (pages 45-65)

Chapter 4 introduces and defines the second pillar, *Set in Order*. It explains why the second pillar is important, and describes problems that are avoided by implementing it. Then it goes through the process of implementing the Set in Order pillar in a company, describing the principles and techniques applied in each step. Some of the principles and techniques taught in this chapter include: the principles of motion economy, the 5S Map, the Signboard Strategy, and the Painting Strategy.

Chapter 5. The Third Pillar: Shine (pages 67-79)

Chapter 5 introduces and defines the third pillar, *Shine*. It explains why the third pillar is important, and describes problems that are avoided by implementing it. It explains how cleaning and inspection are related. Then it goes through the steps for implementing Shine in a company, describing the tools and techniques taught in each step. Some of the tools and techniques taught in this chapter include: 5S Schedules, the Five-minute Shine and creating standards for Shine procedures.

Chapter 6. The Fourth Pillar: Standardize (pages 81-99)

Chapter 6 introduces and defines the fourth pillar, *Standardize*. It explains why the fourth pillar is important, and describes problems that are avoided by implementing it. It also describes how the fourth pillar builds on the first three, creating standards for how the first three pillars will be implemented.

This chapter goes through the steps for implementing the 5S pillar, Standardize, in a company, and describes the tools and techniques applied in each step. Finally, it explains how Standardize can be taken to the higher level of prevention by applying techniques such as suspension and use elimination.

Chapter 7. The Fifth Pillar: Sustain (pages 101-113)

Chapter 7 introduces and defines the fifth pillar, *Sustain*. It explains how the first four pillars cannot be implemented successfully without the commitment to maintain them and describes problems that are avoided by implementing this fifth pillar. It discusses how a company can create the conditions needed to implement the Sustain pillar, and presents the role of management and individuals in maintaining commitment to 5S. Finally, this chapter describes a number of tools that a company can use to sustain the implementation of the five pillars, such as: 5S Slogans, 5S Posters, 5S Photo Exhibits and Storyboards, 5S Newsletters, 5S Pocket Manuals, 5S Department Tours, and 5S Months.

Chapter 8. Reflections and Conclusions (pages 115-119)

Chapter 8 presents reflections on and conclusions to this book. It discusses possibilities for applying what you've learned, and suggests ways for you to create a personal five pillars action plan. It also describes opportunities for further learning about 5S implementation.

In Conclusion

SUMMARY

The author's purpose in writing this book is to give you the information you need to participate in 5S implementation in your company. In order to get the most out of your reading experience, it is also important for you to ask yourself why you are reading this book.

This book is based on Hiroyuki Hirano's book 5 *Pillars of the Visual Workplace*. You can read it on your own or as part of a study group process within your company.

In order to get the most out of your reading it is important to begin by familiarizing yourself with the contents, structure, and design of this book. Then you can follow specific steps for each chapter, which will make your reading more efficient, effective, and enjoyable. This strategy is based on two principles about the way your brain learns:

1) Your brain learns best when it has a framework in which to place new information.

2) It is easier to learn a layer at a time, instead of trying to absorb all the information at once.

Chapter 1, "Getting Started," is the chapter you have just completed. Chapter 2 defines the word "pillar," gives a short explanation of each of the five pillars of 5S, and reviews the benefits of 5S implementation. Chapters 3 through 7 explain the concepts and tools of implementing each of the five pillars: Sort, Set in Order, Shine, Standardize, and Sustain. Chapter 8 presents the conclusions to this book and suggests ways for you to create a personal 5S action plan.

REFLECTIONS

Now that you've completed this chapter, take five minutes to think about these questions and to jot down your answers.

- What did you learn from reading this chapter that stands out as being particularly useful or interesting?
- Do you have any questions about the topics presented in this chapter? If so, what are they?
- What information do you still need to fully understand the ideas presented?
- How can you get this information?

Chapter 2. Introduction and Overview

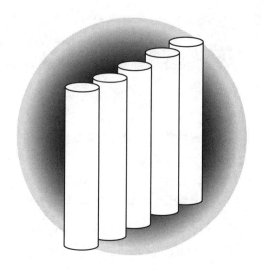

Introduction to the Five Pillars of 5S

Context for Implementing the Five Pillars

Factories are like living organisms. The healthiest organisms move and change in a flexible relationship with their environment.

In the business world, customer needs are always changing, new technologies are continually being developed, and generation after generation of new products appear on the market. Meanwhile, sales competition increases each year as companies strive to manufacture more sophisticated products at lower cost.

Because of these challenges, factories must find new ways to ensure their survival by adapting to the changing business environment. To do this, they must move beyond old organizational concepts and customs that no longer apply and adopt new methods that are appropriate to the times.

Key Point

Thorough implementation of the five pillars of 5S is the starting point in the development of improvement activities to ensure any company's survival. And, of course, survival of the company is necessary in order for the company's employees to keep their jobs.

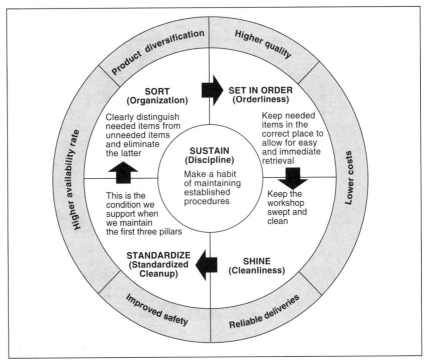

Figure 2-1. The Five Pillars

Overview of the Five Pillars

The word "pillar" is used as a metaphor to mean one of a group of structural elements which together support a structural system. In this case, the five pillars are supporting a system for improvement in your company.

Definition

The five pillars are defined as Sort, Set in Order, Shine, Standardize, and Sustain (see Figure 2-1). Because these words begin with S, they are also referred to as 5S. The two most important elements are Sort and Set in Order. The success of improvement activities depends upon them.

Example

Imagine a factory filled with equipment operators who do not mind working amid dirt, debris, and oil. People working in this factory consider the search for parts, dies, and tools a part of their jobs. Workers who know where to look for missing items are highly valued.

These conditions indicate a factory that produces far too many defective goods, that misses far too many delivery deadlines, and that suffers from low productivity and morale. It is obvious that such a factory has failed to implement the Sort and Set in Order pillars.

13

Figure 2-2. A Disorganized Home Environment

Why the Five Pillars Are the Foundation of 5S Improvement Activities

As we said on the previous page, the five pillars are the foundation of improvement activities. When people first learn about the five pillars it may be hard for them to understand why. Here is an everyday explanation.

Example

People practice the five pillars in their personal lives without even noticing it. We practice Sort and Set in Order when we keep things like wastebaskets, towels, and tissues in convenient and familiar places. When our home environment becomes crowded and disorganized, we tend to function less efficiently (see Figure 2-2).

Key Point

Few factories are as standardized with five-pillar (5S) routines as is the daily life of an orderly person. This is unfortunate since, *in the daily work of a factory, just as in the daily life of a person, routines that maintain organization and orderliness are essential to a smooth and efficient flow of activities.* Sort and Set in Order are in fact the foundation for achieving zero defects, cost reductions, safety improvements, and zero accidents.

Photo 2-1. A Die-cast Factory that Needs to Implement the 5S System

The 5S system sounds so simple that people often dismiss its importance (see Photo 2-1). However the fact remains that

- a neat and clean factory has higher productivity.
- a neat and clean factory produces fewer defects.
- a neat and clean factory meets deadlines better.
- a neat and clean factory is a much safer place to work.

TAKE FIVE

Take five minutes to think about these questions and to jot down your answers.

- What are some of the survival or competition issues that your company is facing?
- What are some of the Sort, Set in Order, and Shine routines that are already part of your daily work life? Your daily personal life?

Photo 2-2. A Messy Pile of Spare Parts

Description of the Five Pillars

The First Pillar: Sort

Definition

Sort means that you remove all items from the workplace that are not needed for current production (or clerical) operations.

Surprisingly, this simple concept is easily misunderstood. At first, it may be difficult to distinguish between what is needed and what is not.

BACKGROUND

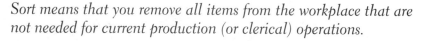

In the beginning, getting rid of items in the workplace can be unnerving. People tend to hang onto parts, thinking that they may be needed for the next order. They see an inappropriate machine and think that they will use it somehow. In this way, inventory and equipment tend to accumulate and get in the way of everyday production activities. This leads to a massive buildup of waste factorywide (see Photos 2-2 and 2-3). In Chapter 3 you will learn to use a "red-tag holding area" to evaluate the necessity of an item instead of simply getting rid of it. This greatly reduces the risk of disposing of an item that is needed later.

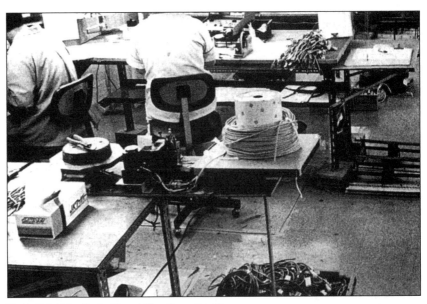

Photo 2-3. Extra Parts Stored Directly on the Floor

Examples of Waste

Example

The following types of waste lead to errors and defects.

- Unneeded inventory creates extra inventory-related costs, such as storage space and management.

- Unneeded transportation of parts requires extra pallets and carts.

- The larger the amount, the harder it is to sort out needed inventory from unneeded inventory.

- Large quantities of stocked items become obsolete due to design changes, limited shelf life, and so on.

- Quality defects result from unneeded in-process inventory and machine breakdowns.

- Unneeded equipment poses a daily obstacle to production activities.

- The presence of unneeded items makes designing equipment layout more difficult.

You will learn more about the first pillar, Sort, in Chapter 3.

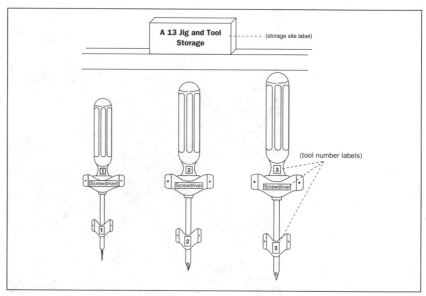

Figure 2-3. Example of Set in Order

The Second Pillar: Set in Order

Definition

Set in Order can be defined as arranging needed items so that they are easy to use and labeling them so that they are easy to find and put away. Set in Order should always be implemented with Sort. Once everything is sorted through, only what is necessary remains. Next it should be made clear where these things belong so that anyone can immediately understand where to find them and where to return them. (See Figure 2-3 for an example of Set in Order).

The Third Pillar: Shine

Definition

The third pillar is Shine. Shine means sweeping floors, wiping off machinery, and generally making sure that everything in the factory stays clean. In a manufacturing company, Shine is closely related to the ability to turn out quality products. Shine also includes saving labor by finding ways to prevent dirt, dust, and debris from piling up in the workshop.

Shine should be integrated into daily maintenance tasks to combine cleaning checkpoints with maintenance checkpoints.

The Fourth Pillar: Standardize

Standardize differs from Sort, Set in Order, and Shine. These first three pillars can be thought of as activities, as something we

Definition

do. In contrast, Standardize is *the method you use to maintain the first three pillars—Sort, Set in Order, and Shine.*

Standardize is related to each of the first three pillars, but it relates most strongly to Shine. It results when we keep machines and their surroundings free of debris, oil, and dirt. It is the condition that exists after we have practiced Shine for some time.

The Fifth Pillar: Sustain

Definition

Within the context of the five pillars, Sustain means *making a habit of properly maintaining correct procedures.*

The first four pillars can be implemented without difficulty if the workplace is one where the employees commit to sustaining 5S conditions. Such a workplace is likely to enjoy high productivity and high quality.

Key Point

In many factories great amounts of time and effort are spent in vain on sorting and cleaning because the company lacks the discipline to maintain 5S conditions and continue 5S implementation on a daily basis. Even if the company occasionally organizes 5S campaigns and contests, *without the Sustain pillar the other pillars will not last long.*

TAKE FIVE

Take five minutes to think about these questions and to jot down your answers.

- Visualize your workplace.
    - Think of one item you could get rid of.
    - Think of one item you could relocate to use more efficiently.
    - Think of one item or area that would benefit from cleaning.
    - Think of one regular routine you could create for getting rid of, relocating, or cleaning items in your work area.
    - Think of some conditions you could create that would promote your carrying out this routine.

Resistance #1	"What's so great about Sort and Set in Order?"
Resistance #2	"Why clean when it just gets dirty again?"
Resistance #3	"Sorting and Setting in Order will not boost output."
Resistance #4	"We already implemented Sort and Set in Order."
Resistance #5	"We did 5S years ago."
Resistance #6	"We're too busy for 5S activities."
Resistance #7	"Why do we need to implement the five pillars?

Figure 2-4. Common Resistances to 5S Implementation

Common Types of Resistance to 5S Implementation

Introduction

Key Point

Any company introducing the five pillars of 5S is likely to encounter resistance (see Figure 2-4). Some common types of resistance are discussed below.

Resistance 1. What's So Great about Sort and Set in Order?

Sort and Set in Order seem so simple that it's hard to believe just how important and powerful they are! The fact remains that 5S implementation is needed when the factory is not neat and organized.

Resistance 2. Why Clean When It Just Gets Dirty Again?

Sometimes people accept dirtiness as an inevitable condition in their workplace. They say that cleaning it up would do little good since it would soon get dirty again. This logic doesn't hold, however, when we look at the negative impact of a dirty workplace on the quality and efficiency of the work.

Resistance 3. Sorting and Setting in Order Will Not Boost Output.

Production workers sometimes assume their job is to make things, not organize or clean things. This way of thinking is understandable if their job has never before included these functions. However, it is an attitude that needs to change as workers come to understand how important the Sort, Set in Order, and Shine activities are to maximizing output.

Resistance 4. We Already Implemented Sort and Set in Order.

Some people consider only the superficial and visible aspects of the five pillars. They think that rearranging things a little and putting them into neat rows is all there is to it. However, such "orderliness" only scratches the surface of what five pillars is all about.

Resistance 5. We Did 5S Years Ago.

This type of comment is heard most often from people who think the five pillar movement is a fad. If they attempted 5S implementation once 20 years ago, they don't see why they should do it again. The five pillars are not a passing fashion. They are actually the fertilizer on the field of making all types of improvements.

Resistance 6. We're Too Busy for 5S Activities

In some workplaces, Sort, Set in Order, and Shine are the first things passed over when work gets busy. The explanation is that "we're too busy for that." It is true that production priorities are sometimes so pressing that other activities need to wait. However, 5S activities are as fundamental to daily life in the factory as washing our faces or brushing our teeth in our personal lives. We may be able to put these activities off for a short time, under certain circumstances. But putting them off longer than that quickly has negative consequences.

Resistance 7. Why Do We Need to Implement the Five Pillars?

It can be difficult to implement the five pillars or other improvement programs at companies that are currently profitable. If you tell people that it is more efficient to keep only one box of parts on hand at each operation, they may respond by saying "Yes, but we're doing all right, and this is the way we've always done it."

Key Point

These types of resistance are common in the early stages of 5S implementation. *If we ignore such resistance and plow ahead with implementation, the result is likely to be nothing more than superficial improvements.* Instead, we need to address these concerns directly. In order for the five pillars to work, everyone needs to truly understand just how necessary they are.

Figure 2-5. Providing Creative Input to Workplace Design

Benefits of 5S Implementation

Benefits to You

Key Point

So what can the implementation of the five pillars of 5S do for you? *It should have many benefits for you.* It will

- give you an opportunity to provide creative input regarding how your workplace should be organized and laid out and how your work should be done (see Figure 2-5).
- make your workplace more pleasant to work in.
- make your job more satisfying.
- remove many obstacles and frustrations in your work.
- help you know what you are expected to do, and when and where you are expected to do it.
- make it easier to communicate with everyone you work with.

Benefits to Your Company

Key Point

Your company will also experience many benefits from implementing the five pillars, such as increasing product diversity, raising quality, lowering costs, encouraging reliable deliveries, promoting safety, building customer confidence, and promoting corporate growth (see Figure 2-6).

22

Benefit 1. Zero Changeovers Bring Product Diversification

Benefit 2. Zero Defects Bring Higher Quality

Benefit 3. Zero Waste Brings Lower Costs

Benefit 4. Zero Delays Bring Reliable Deliveries

Benefit 5. Zero Injuries Promote Safety

Benefit 6. Zero Breakdowns Bring Better Equipment Availability

Benefit 7. Zero Complaints Bring Greater Confidence and Trust

Benefit 8. Zero Red Ink Brings Corporate Growth

Figure 2-6. Benefits to Your Company

Benefit 1. Zero Changeovers Bring Product Diversification

To remain competitive companies must reduce changeover time to zero, increase changeover frequency, and become more adaptive to product diversification. The five pillars help reduce changeover time by reducing searching time and raising overall operating efficiency.

Benefit 2. Zero Defects Bring Higher Quality

Defects result from many causes, including attaching the wrong parts and using the wrong jig. Sort and Set in Order prevent these kinds of errors. Further, keeping production equipment clean reduces equipment-operation errors and enables faster retooling. These and other effects of 5S implementation all add up to fewer defects.

Benefit 3. Zero Waste Brings Lower Costs

Factories and offices are virtual storehouses of waste. 5S implementation can help eliminate the following types of waste:

- in-process and warehouse inventory
- the use of excessive amounts of space for storage
- stand-by waste while waiting for equipment to transport items
- searching waste, when necessary items are hard to find
- motion waste, in side-stepping poorly located equipment and supplies

Figure 2-7. Zero Delays Promote Reliable Deliveries

Benefit 4. Zero Delays Bring Reliable Deliveries

Factories that lack thorough 5S implementation tend to produce defects no matter what they do to prevent them. Deadlines whiz by while everyone is busy reworking defective products. It is difficult to meet delivery deadlines in the face of problems like wasteful motion and too many errors and defects. When these problems are eliminated, deliveries become more reliable (see Figure 2-7).

Benefit 5. Zero Injuries Promote Safety

Injuries can be expected when items are left in walkways, when stock is piled high in storage areas, or when equipment is covered with grime, cutting shavings, or oil.

Benefit 6. Zero Breakdowns Bring Better Equipment Availability

When daily maintenance tasks are integrated with daily cleaning tasks, operators notice problems before they cause a breakdown. In this way, equipment is more consistently ready for use. Clean, well-maintained equipment breaks down less frequently and is also easier to diagnose and repair when breakdowns do occur.

Benefit 7. Zero Complaints Bring Greater Confidence and Trust

Factories that practice the five pillars are virtually free of defects and delays. This means they are also free of customer complaints about product quality.

- Products from a neat and clean workshop are defect-free.

- Products from a neat and clean workshop cost less to make.

- Products from a neat and clean workshop arrive on time.

- Products from a neat and clean workshop are safe.

Benefit 8. Zero Red Ink Brings Corporate Growth

Companies cannot grow without the trust of customers.
The five pillars provide a strong base upon which to build customer trust and loyalty. Therefore, factories with a solid 5S foundation are more likely to grow.

TAKE FIVE

Take five minutes to think about these questions and to jot down your answers.

- What are some of the benefits you might experience from 5S implementation in your workplace?

- What are some of the companywide benefits that might be experienced from implementation of the 5S's?

In Conclusion

SUMMARY

The word "pillar" is used as a metaphor to mean one of a group of structural elements that together support a structural system. In this case, the five pillars of 5S are supporting a system for improvement in your company.

The five pillars are Sort, Set in Order, Shine, Standardize, and Sustain. In any company, thorough implementation of the five pillars is the starting point for improvement activities that will ensure survival. This is because, in the daily work of a factory, just as in our daily lives, we perform routines that Sort, Set in Order, and Shine; these are essential to a smooth and efficient flow of activities.

Sort means removing from the workplace all items that are not needed for current production operations. Set in Order means arranging needed items so that they are easy to use and labeling them so that they are easy to find and put away. Shine means sweeping floors, wiping off machinery, and generally making sure that everything in the factory stays clean. Standardize is the method for maintaining the first three pillars. Sustain means making a habit of properly maintaining correct procedures.

When the five pillars are first implemented, it is inevitable that certain types of resistance will arise. Some of these include lack of understanding about why the five pillars are so important, reluctance to clean since things will get dirty again, and the belief that work is too busy to take time out to organize, order, and clean the workplace. This resistance can derail your company's efforts at 5S implementation if it is not addressed directly and carefully.

There are many benefits of implementing the five pillars of 5S. The benefits to you personally include a more pleasant workplace, greater job satisfaction, and an opportunity to provide creative input to the way your work should be done. The benefits to your company include higher product quality, lower costs, increased customer satisfaction, and corporate growth.

REFLECTIONS

Now that you've completed this chapter, take five minutes to think about these questions and to jot down your answers.

- What did you learn from reading this chapter that stands out as being particularly useful or interesting?
- Do you have any questions about the topics presented in this chapter? If so, what are they?
- What do you still need information about in order to fully understand the ideas presented?
- How can you get this information?

Chapter 3. The First Pillar: Sort

CHAPTER OVERVIEW

Explanation of the First Pillar—Sort

- Introduction
- Definition of the First Pillar
- The Key to the First Pillar
- Why Sort Is Important
- Problems Avoided by Implementing Sort

How to Implement Sort

- Introduction
- Overview of Red-Tagging
- Red-Tag Holding Areas
- Local vs. Central Red-Tag Holding Areas

Steps in Red-Tagging

- Overview
- Step 1: Launch the Red-Tag Project
- Step 2: Identify Red-Tag Targets
- Step 3: Set Red-Tag Criteria
- Step 4: Make Red Tags
- Step 5: Attach the Red Tags
- Step 6: Evaluate the Red-Tagged Items
- Step 7: Document the Results of Red-Tagging
- When Red-Tagging Is Completed

Accumulation of Unneeded Items

- Introduction
- Types of Unneeded Items
- Places Where Unneeded Items Accumulate

Red-Tagging Suggestions and Reminders

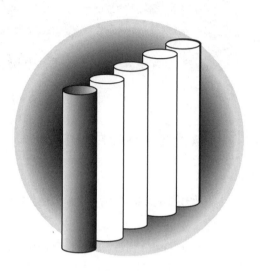

Explanation of the First Pillar—Sort

Introduction

We start learning early about getting things organized and sorted. As children, we were told to organize (sort) our toys and books. Strictly speaking, this kind of organizing is not the same as that practiced as part of the five pillars. When children organize their toys and books, they usually line them up or store them some-where—without sorting out what is necessary (and to be kept) from what is unnecessary (and to be discarded).

Definition of the First Pillar

Definition

Sort, the first pillar of the visual workplace, corresponds to the just-in-time (JIT) principle of "only what is needed, only in the amounts needed, and only when it is needed." In other words, *Sort means that you remove all items from the workplace that are not needed for current production (or clerical) operations.*

The Key to the First Pillar

Key Point

Sort does not mean that you throw out only items that you are sure you will never need. Nor does it mean that you simply arrange things into neat, straight patterns. *If you Sort, you leave only the bare essentials: When in doubt, throw it out. This principle is a key part of Sort in the context of the five pillars.*

Why Sort is Important

Key Point

Implementing this first pillar creates a work environment in which space, time, money, energy, and other resources can be managed and used most effectively. *When the first pillar is well implemented, problems and annoyances in the work flow are reduced, communication between workers is improved, product quality is increased, and productivity is enhanced.*

Problems Avoided by Implementing Sort

When the first pillar is not well implemented, the following types of problems tend to arise:

1. The factory becomes increasingly crowded and hard to work in.

2. Lockers, shelves, and cabinets for storage of unneeded items put walls between employees, getting in the way of communication.

3. Time is wasted in searching for parts and tools.

4. Unneeded inventory and machinery are costly to maintain.

5. Excess stock-on-hand hides other types of problems in production.

6. Unneeded items and equipment make it harder to improve the process flow.

TAKE FIVE

Take five minutes to think about this question and to jot down your answer.

- What problems occur in your work area because of the accumulation of unneeded items?

Photo 3-1: Examples of Red-Tagged Items

How to Implement Sort

New Tool

Introduction

It is not always easy to identify unneeded items in the factory. Workers seldom know how to separate items needed for current production from unnecessary items. Factory managers often see factory waste without recognizing it.

The Red-Tag Strategy is a simple method for identifying potentially unneeded items in the factory, evaluating their usefulness, and dealing with them appropriately

Overview of Red-Tagging

Red-tagging literally means putting red tags on items in the factory that need to be evaluated as being necessary or unnecessary (see Photo 3-1). The red tags catch people's attention because red is a color that stands out. An item with a red tag is asking three questions:

- Is this item needed?

- If it is needed, is it needed in this quantity?

- If it is needed, does it need to be located here?

Once these items are identified, they can be evaluated and dealt with appropriately. They may be

- held in a "Red-Tag Holding Area" for a period of time to see whether they are needed,

- disposed of,

- relocated,

- left exactly where they are

Red-Tag Holding Areas

New Tool

In order to implement the red-tag strategy effectively, a red-tag holding area must be created. A red-tag holding area is an area set aside for use in storing red-tagged items that need further evaluation. It gives you a safety net between first questioning whether something is needed, and actually getting rid of that item. This buffer is helpful when the need or frequency of need for that item is unknown.

Key Point

In other cases, the red-tag holding area can serve as an emotional buffer when people are concerned about getting rid of things. Sometimes we are concerned about giving up something we think we may need later. *When an item is set aside and watched for an agreed-upon period of time people tend to be more ready to let it go when that time is over.*

Local vs. Central Red-Tag Holding Areas

Key Point

Usually an organization that is launching a companywide red-tagging effort needs to establish a central red-tag holding area. This area is used to manage the flow of items that cannot or should not be disposed of by individual departments or production areas.

Key Point

Each department or production area that participates in red-tagging also needs a local red-tag holding area. The local red-tag holding area is used to manage the flow of red-tagged items within a local department or production area.

Steps in Red-Tagging

How-to Steps

Overview

The red-tagging process in a department or work area can be broken down into seven steps.

Step 1: Launch the red-tag project.

Step 2: Identify the red-tag targets.

Step 3: Set red-tag criteria.

Step 4: Make red tags.

Step 5: Attach red tags.

Step 6: Evaluate red-tagged items.

Step 7: Document the results of red-tagging.

Step 1: Launch the Red-Tag Project

In general, red-tag campaigns are started and coordinated by the upper-level management of a company. Even when a red-tag campaign is companywide, local campaigns need to be organized in each department or production area. This involves

- organizing a team*
- organizing supplies
- organizing a time or schedule to perform red-tagging
- setting aside a local red-tag holding area
- planning for disposal of red-tagged items

*People from outside a department can be valuable members on a red-tagging team since they tend to see the area with a fresh eye. Because of this, it is helpful to partner with other departments or production areas in creating red-tagging teams.

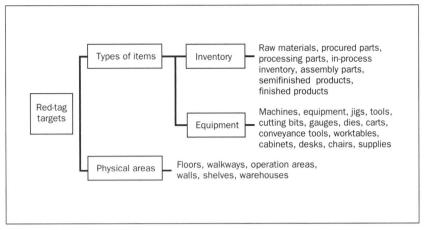

Figure 3-1. Identifying Red-Tag Targets

Step 2: Identify Red-Tag Targets

Key Point

Identifying red-tag targets means identifying two things (see Figure 3-1).

(a) the specific types of items to evaluate

In the manufacturing area, the targets for red tags include: inventory, equipment, and space. Inventory can be divided into warehouse inventory and in-process inventory. Warehouse inventory has its own subdivisions: material, parts, products, and so on.

(b) the physical areas where red-tagging will take place

It is better to define a smaller area and evaluate it well than to define a larger area and not be able to evaluate it fully in the time available.

TAKE FIVE

Take five minutes to think about these questions and to jot down your answers.

- Name three types of items that you could target for red-tagging in your workplace.
- Name three physical areas in your workplace that could be targeted for red-tagging.

Step 3. Set Red-Tag Criteria

As we have already discussed, the most difficult thing about red-tagging is differentiating what is needed from what is not. This issue can be managed by establishing clear-cut criteria for what is needed in a particular area and what is not. The most common criterion is the next month's production schedule.

- Items needed for that schedule are kept in that location.

- Items not needed for the schedule can be disposed of or stored in a separate location.

Key Point

This discussion shows that three main factors determine whether an item is necessary or not. These factors are:

- *The usefulness of the item to perform the work at hand*
   - If the item isn't needed it should be disposed of.

- *The frequency with which the item is needed*
   - If it is needed infrequently it can be stored away from the work area.

- *The quantity of the item needed to perform this work*
   - If it is needed in limited quantity the excess can be disposed of or stored away from the work area.

In the final analysis, each company must establish its own red-tagging criteria—and each department may customize this standard to meet its local needs.

Step 4. Make Red Tags

Key Point

Each company has specific needs for documenting and reporting the movement, use, and value of materials, equipment, tools, inventory, and products (see step 7 on page 39). *The company's red tags should be designed to support this documentation process.*

Various types of information on a red tag may include:

- Category. Provides a general idea of the type of item (e.g., a warehouse item or machine). Categories include raw materials, in-process inventory, products, equipment, jigs, tools, and dies.

- Item name and manufacturing number.

- Quantity. Indicates the number of items included under this red tag.

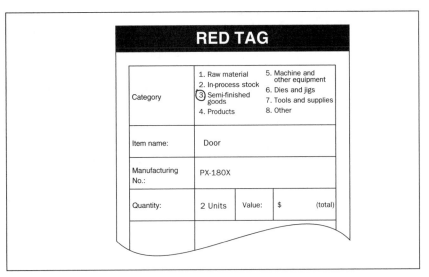

Figure 3-2. Example of a Red Tag

- Reasons. Describes why a red tag has been attached to this item.

- Division. Includes the name of the division responsible for managing the red-tagged item.

- Value. Includes the value of the red-tagged item.

- Date. Includes the red-tagging date.

The material used for red tags can be red paper, thick red tape, or whatever else works. Red tags can be laminated with plastic or another material to protect them during repeated use. (See Figure 3-2 for an example of a red tag.)

Step 5. Attach the Red Tags

Key Point

The best way to carry out red-tagging is to do the whole target area quickly—if possible, in one or two days. In fact, many companies choose to red-tag their entire factory during a one- or two-day period. Red-tagging should be a short and powerful event.

At this stage in the game you should red-tag all items you question, without evaluating what to do with them. Refer to pages 40 and 41 in this chapter for tips on spotting unneeded items.

Treatment	Description
Throw it away	Dispose of as scrap or incinerate items that are useless or unneeded for any purpose.
Sell	Sell off to other companies items that are useless or unneeded for any purpose.
Return	Return items to the supply company.
Lend out	Lend items to other sections of the company that can use them on a temporary basis.
Distribute	Distribute items to another part of the company on a permanent basis.
Central red-tag area	Send items to the central red-tag holding area for redistribution, storage, or disposal.

Table 3-1. Disposal Methods

Step 6. Evaluate the Red-Tagged Items

Key Point

In this step the red-tag criteria established in step 3 are used to evaluate what to do with red-tagged items. Options include:

- Keep the item where it is.
- Move the item to a new location in the work area.
- Store the item away from the work area.
- Hold the item in the local red-tag holding area for evaluation.
- Dispose of the item.

Disposal methods include (see Table 3-1):

- Throw it away.
- Sell it.
- Return it to the vendor.
- Lend it out.
- Distribute it to a different part of the company.
- Send it to the central red-tag holding area.

A Note about Large Equipment

As a target for red-tagging, equipment is as important as inventory. Ideally, unnecessary equipment should be removed from areas where daily production activities take place.

However, large equipment and equipment attached to the floor may be expensive to move. It is sometimes better to leave this equipment where it is unless it interferes with daily production activities or prevents workshop improvements. In the meantime, label unneeded equipment with a "freeze" red tag, which indicates that its use has been "frozen," but that it will remain in place for the time being.

Step 7: Document the Results of Red-Tagging

Key Point

As explained earlier, each company has its own needs for documenting and reporting the movement, use, and value of materials, equipment, tools, inventory, and products. *Because of this, each company needs to create its own system for logging and tracking necessary information as red-tagging takes place.* The system may involve a written logbook in each department and in the central red-tag holding area. Or, it may involve entering data from the red tags into a computer system.

Key Point

Whatever the system, documenting results is an important part of the red-tagging process. It allows the company to measure the improvements and savings produced as a result of the red-tagging effort. As we indicated in Step 4, your company's red tags should be designed to support the documentation process it decides to use.

When Red-Tagging Is Completed

When red-tagging is completed the factory is usually dotted with empty spaces—a sign of real progress. Now the layout of equipment and worktables can be changed to take advantage of the added space. This is part of the second pillar, Set in Order.

Often companies that think they need to build a new factory to turn out new products discover plenty of space when they use the red-tag strategy.

TAKE FIVE

Take five minutes to think about this question and to jot down your answer.

- What would be an appropriate red-tagging criteria for your workplace? (Note: This criteria should address the three main factors of "need" for an item: usefulness, frequency of need, and quantity needed).

Photo 3-2. Disorderly Piles Line the Wall

Accumulation of Unneeded Items

Introduction

Key Point

Certain types of unneeded items tend to accumulate in factories and warehouses in predictable places. This section gives some pointers about the types of unneeded items that accumulate in factories and warehouses, and where these items are often found.

Types of Unneeded Items

Here are some types of unneeded items that tend to accumulate:

- defective or excess quantities of small parts and inventory
- outdated or broken jigs and dies
- worn-out bits
- outdated or broken tools and inspection gear
- old rags and other cleaning supplies
- electrical equipment with broken cords
- outdated posters, signs, notices, and memos

Places Where Unneeded Items Accumulate

Here are some locations where unneeded items tend to accumulate:

- in rooms or areas not designated for any particular purpose
- in corners next to entrances or exits
- along interior and exterior walls, next to partitions, and behind pillars (see Photo 3-2)
- under the eaves of warehouses
- under desks and shelves and in desk and cabinet drawers
- near the bottom of tall stacks of items
- on unused management and production schedule boards
- in tool boxes that are not clearly sorted

Red-Tagging Suggestions and Reminders

If done correctly, red-tagging can produce impressive results for your company. To help you get the most out of your red-tagging efforts we offer the following suggestions and reminders:

Set a Target Number of Red Tags to Be Used

Instead of handing them out as needed, determine in advance approximately how many red tags each workplace should use. Experience shows that we can expect an average of four red tags per workshop employee. In other words, a workshop with 30 employees should need about 120 red tags.

Apply One Red Tag per Item

When finding a shelf full of odds and ends, it is tempting to attach one red tag for the whole shelf. However, this can lead to confusion when it is time to dispose of these shelved items. Avoid this temptation and attach individual tags to individual items.

Red-Tag Excess Needed Items

We obviously want to red-tag items that are unneeded. However, we should also red-tag items that are needed—if there are excessive amounts of them. Required amounts can be calculated based on the red-tagging criteria that has been set by the company or the department (see step 3, page 36). Everything in excess of these amounts should be removed from the workplace.

In Conclusion

SUMMARY

The first pillar is Sort, which means that you remove all items from the workplace that are not needed for current production. When in doubt, throw it out. When the first pillar is well implemented, problems and annoyances in the work flow are reduced, communication between workers is improved, product quality is increased, and productivity is enhanced.

The Red-Tag Strategy is a simple method for identifying potentially unneeded items in the factory or warehouse, evaluating whether they are needed, and dealing with them appropriately. In order to implement red-tagging effectively, a red-tag holding area must be created. A red-tag holding area is an area set aside for use in storing red-tagged items that need further evaluation. When an item is set aside and watched for an agreed-upon period of time, people tend to be more ready to let it go when that time is over.

Usually an organization launching a companywide red-tagging effort needs to establish a central red-tag holding area to manage the flow of items that cannot be disposed of by individual departments. Each department or production area that participates in red-tagging also needs a local red-tag holding area to manage the flow of red-tagged items within the department or local production area.

There are seven steps in the red-tagging process. Step 1 is launching the red-tagging project in the department or throughout the company. Step 2 involves identifying red-tagging targets. This means identifying the types of items and the physical work areas to be evaluated. Step 3 is setting red-tagging criteria. There are three main factors in this criteria: the usefulness of the item to perform the work at hand; the frequency with which the item is needed; and the quantity of the item needed to perform the work. Step 4 is making the red tags. Red tags should be designed to support the company's process for documenting and reporting red-tagging results.

Step 5 is attaching the red tags. The best way to carry out red-tagging is to do the whole target area quickly— if possible in one or two days. Step 6 is evaluating red-tagged items. Here the red-tagging criteria is used to evaluate what to do with red-tagged items. Finally, in step 7, the results of red-tagging are documented. Each company will have its own needs for documenting and reporting the movement, use, and value of equipment, tools, and inventory. Because of this, each company needs to create its own system for logging and tracking red-tagging information.

When carrying out step 5, it is important to be on the alert for certain types of items that tend to accumulate in factories and warehouses in predictable places. For your company to get the most out of its red-tagging efforts it is also important to set a target number of red tags to be used; apply one red tag per item; and tag excess amounts of needed items.

REFLECTIONS

Now that you've completed this chapter, take five minutes to think about these questions and to jot down your answers.

- What did you learn from reading this chapter that stands out as being particularly useful or interesting?

- Do you have any questions about the topics presented in this chapter? If so, what are they?

- What information do you still need to fully understand the ideas presented?

- How can you get this information?

Chapter 4. The Second Pillar: Set in Order

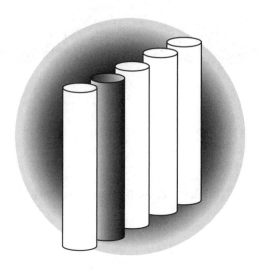

Explanation of the Second Pillar—Set in Order

Introduction

In Chapter 3 you learned about the first pillar, Sort. The second pillar, Set in Order, can be implemented only when the first pillar is in place. No matter how well you arrange items, Set in Order can have little impact if many of the items are unnecessary. Similarly, if sorting is implemented without Setting in Order, it is much less effective. *Sort and Set in Order work best when they are implemented together.*

Key Point

Definition of the Second Pillar

Definition

Set in Order means that you arrange needed items so that they are easy to use and label them so that anyone can find them and put them away. The key word in this definition is "anyone."

Why Set in Order Is Important

Key Point

Setting in Order is important because it eliminates many kinds of waste in production or clerical activities. These include searching waste, waste due to difficulty in using items, and waste due to difficulty in returning items.

Example

Both factories and offices have more than their share of searching waste. For example, it is not unusual for a three-hour changeover routine to include 30 minutes of searching. When attempting to reduce changeover time radically (for example, from 3 hours to just 10 minutes), there is clearly no room for 30 minutes of searching waste.

Problems Avoided by Implementing Set in Order

Examples

The following list gives examples of the types of waste and the kinds of problems that are avoided when Set in Order activities are well implemented:

1. Motion Waste: The person sent to get a cart could not find it.

2. Searching Waste: No one can find the key to the locked cabinet that contains needed tools.

3. The Waste of Human Energy: A frustrated worker gives up on finding a needed template after looking in vain for half an hour.

4. The Waste of Excess Inventory: Desk drawers are crammed full of pencils, markers, and other stationery supplies.

5. The Waste of Defective Products: The storage locations of two types of parts are switched without telling the operator, so he picks up the wrong part without noticing and uses it in the product.

6. The Waste of Unsafe Conditions: Boxes of supplies are left in a walkway, causing someone to trip and get injured.

Definition of Standardization

Definition

Standardization means creating a consistent way that tasks and procedures are carried out. When we think "standardization," we should think "anyone." Machinery standardization means anyone can operate the machinery. Operation standardization means anyone can perform the operation. To get along together, we even need to standardize our behavior to a certain extent— although, of course, we always keep our individuality.

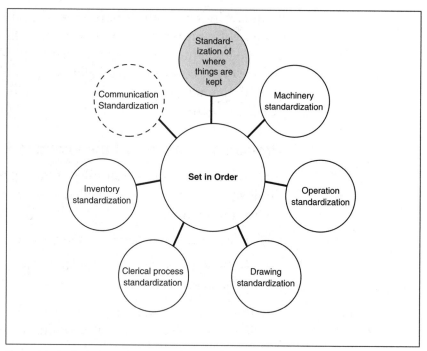

Figure 4-1. Set in Order Is the Core of Standardization

Set in Order Is the Core of Standardization

Key Point

The Set in Order pillar is the core of standardization (see Figure 4-1). This is because the workplace must be orderly before any type of standardization can be implemented effectively.

The Concept of Visual Controls

Definition

Understanding where things are kept brings us to the concept of visual control. *A visual control is any communication device used in the work environment that tells us at a glance how work should be done.* Visual controls are used to communicate information such as where items belong (see Photo 4-1); how many items belong there; what the standard procedure is for doing something; the status of work in process; and many other types of information critical to the flow of work activities.

Key Point

In any situation, we can implement standardization in such a way that all standards are identified by visual controls. When this happens, there is only one place to put each item, and we can

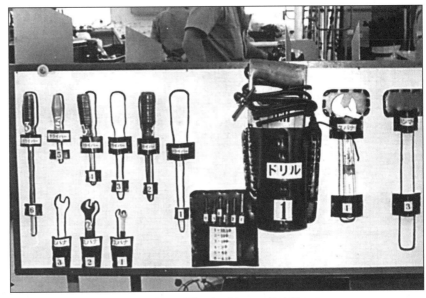

Photo 4-1. Example of a Visual Control Used to Manage Tool Storage

tell right away whether a particular operation is proceeding normally or abnormally.

In the Set in Order pillar, we use visual controls to communicate standards related to where items belong. Be sure to notice how the methods described in the rest of the chapter use visual controls.

TAKE FIVE

Take five minutes to think about these questions and to jot down your answers.

1. What are three examples of visual controls that already exist in your workplace?

2. Give one example of each type of waste listed in this section that you see in your workplace.

How to Implement Set in Order

Introduction

In this section you'll learn two steps to Set in Order.

How-to Steps

Step One: You'll learn some principles for deciding best locations for jigs, tools, parts, equipment, and machinery. Then you'll learn a tool called the 5S Map which is helpful in evaluating current locations, and deciding best locations.

Step Two: You'll learn how to identify these best locations once they have been decided.

Step One: Deciding Appropriate Locations

The 5S Map takes you through a step-by-step process for evaluating current locations and deciding best locations. Before you begin learning about the 5S Map, however, it is important for you to learn some basic principles of why certain locations are better than others.

BACKGROUND

Principle

Principles of Storing Jigs, Tools, and Dies to Eliminate Waste

The first set of principles applies to finding the best locations for jigs, tools, and dies. These items differ from materials and parts in that they must be put back after each use. However, some of these principles also apply to parts, equipment, and machinery. They say you should

- Locate items in the workplace according to their frequency of use.
  - Place frequently used items near the place of use.
  - Store infrequently used items away from the place of use.

- Store items together if they are used together, and store them in the sequence in which they are used (see figure 4-3).

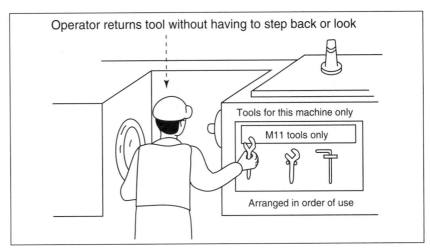

Figure 4-3. Tools Kept Close at Hand and Stored in the Order Used

- Devise a "just let go" arrangement for tools. This approach involves suspending tools from a retractable cord just within reach so that they will automatically go back into their correct storage position when released.

- Make storage places larger than the items stored there so that they are physically easy to remove and put back.

- Eliminate the variety of jigs, tools, and dies needed by creating a few jigs, tools, and dies that serve multiple functions.

- Store tools according to function or product:
  - Function-based storage means storing tools together when they have similar functions. This works best for job-shop production.
  - Product-based storage means storing tools together when they are used on the same product. This works best for repetitive production.

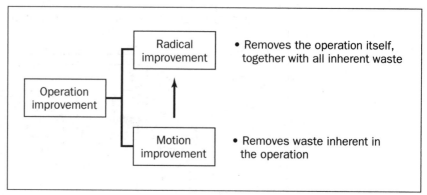

Figure 4-4. Radical Improvement and Motion Improvement

Principles of Motion Economy to Eliminate Waste

Another set of principles is helpful in deciding the best locations for parts, equipment, and machinery, as well as tools. It focuses on removing waste from human motions. By this we mean the waste of time, energy, and effort when people have to move their trunks, feet, arms, and hands more than is absolutely necessary to perform a given operation. *By locating parts, equipment, machinery, and tools in the best locations possible, we can minimize motion waste.*

Key Point

Even more important than removing motion waste is asking why it occurs. By asking "why" we can find methods of manufacturing that approach the zero-waste mark.

Definitions

Clearly, the process of *removing motion waste involves eliminating unnecessary motion from existing operations. This is called "motion improvement." The process of removing waste may also involve finding ways to eliminate whole operations. This is called "radical improvement"*(see Figure 4-4).

Principles

The principles listed below help us either to eliminate or to reduce the motions that operators make.

Principle 1: Start and end each motion with both hands moving at once.

Principle 2: Both arms should move symmetrically and in opposite directions.

Principle 3: Keep trunk motions to a minimum.

Principle 4: Use gravity instead of muscle.

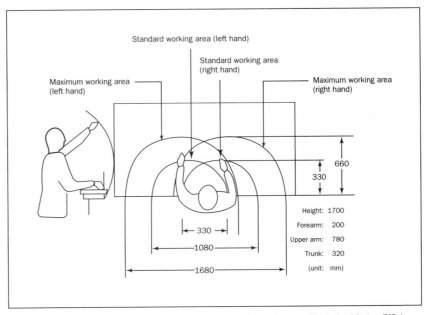

Figure 4-5. Guidelines for Locating Parts, Equipment, and Machinery to Maximize Motion Efficiency

Principle 5: Avoid zigzagging motions and sudden changes in direction.

Principle 6: Move with a steady rhythm.

Principle 7: Maintain a comfortable posture with comfortable motions.

Principle 8: Use the feet to operate on and off switches for machines where practical.

Principle 9: Keep materials and tools close and in front (see Figure 4-5).

Principle 10: Arrange materials and tools in the order of their use.

Principle 11: Use inexpensive methods for feeding in and sending out materials.

Principle 12: Stand at a proper height for the work to be done.

Principle 13: Make materials and parts easy to pick up.

Principle 14: Make handles and grips in efficient, easy-to-use shapes and positions.

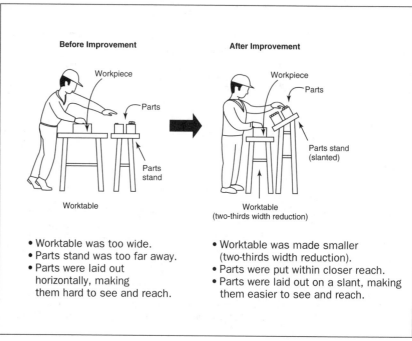

Figure 4-6. Improvement in Picking up Parts

Examples of Eliminating Motion Waste

Example

Improving the Retrieval of Parts

Figure 4-6 shows an improvement in picking up parts as part of assembly work. Before this improvement, the worktable was so large that the assembly worker had to stretch to pick up parts. Also, the parts boxes were laid flat at table level, making it difficult to reach inside them.

After the improvement, the decreased width of the worktable enabled the assembly worker to reach the parts without stretching his arm too far. Furthermore, the parts boxes were set on an inclined surface to make their contents more accessible.

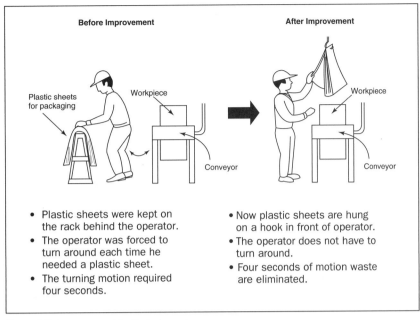

Figure 4-7. Improvement in Parts Layout

Example

Improving the Layout of Parts

Figure 4-7 shows an improvement in how plastic packaging sheets are used. The sheets are moved from a rack behind the operator to a hook in front of the operator and above the production line. This improvement eliminates four seconds of motion waste from each unit of packaging work.

TAKE FIVE

Take five minutes to think about these questions and to jot down your answers.

- Identify two examples of how you could apply the principles of storing jigs, tools, and dies to eliminate waste in your own work.

- Identify two examples of how you could apply the principles of motion economy to eliminate waste in your own work.

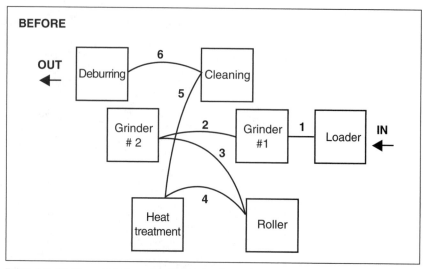

Figure 4-8. 5S Map of Old Layout in Machining Operations

Using the 5S Map to Decide Locations

New Tool

The 5S Map is a tool that can be used to evaluate current locations of parts, jigs, tools, dies, equipment, and machinery, and to decide best locations. Using the 5S Map actually involves creating two maps—a "before" map and an "after" map. The "before" map shows the layout of parts, jigs, tools, dies, equipment, and machinery in the workplace before you Set in Order. The "after" map shows the layout of parts, jigs, tools, dies, equipment, and machinery in the workplace after you implement Set in Order. The "after" map will be discussed later in this chapter.

The 5S Map can be used to evaluate orderliness in small or large work areas, for example, in a single workstation, on a production line, or in a department. Here are the steps to creating and using a 5S Map.

How-to Steps

1. Make a floor plan or area diagram of the work space you wish to study. Show the location of specific parts inventory, tools, jigs, dies, equipment, and machinery.

2. Draw arrows on the plan showing the work flow between items in the work space. There should be at least one arrow for every operation performed. Draw the arrows in the order that the operations are performed, and number them as you go (see Figure 4-8).

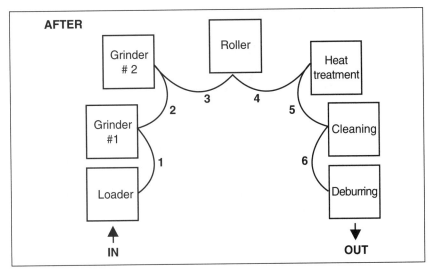

Figure 4-9. 5S Map of New Layout in Machining Operations

3. Look carefully at the resulting "spaghetti diagram." It is a "before" map that shows work space layout before Set in Order is implemented. Can you see places where there is congestion in the work flow? According to the principles presented earlier in this chapter, can you see ways to eliminate waste?

4. Make a new 5S Map to experiment with a better layout for this work space. Again, draw and number arrows to show the flow of operations performed.

5. Analyze the efficiency of this layout, using the principles we have already discussed.

6. Continue to experiment with possible layouts using the 5S Map until you find one you think will work well (see Figure 4-9).

7. Implement this new layout in the work space, moving parts, tools, jigs, dies, equipment, and machinery to their new locations.

8. Continue to evaluate and improve the orderliness of the layout in the work space.

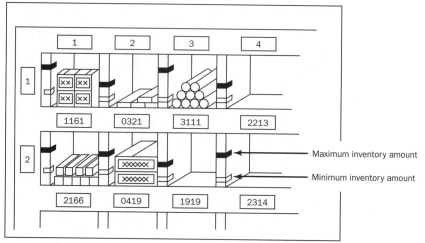

Maximum inventory amount

Minimum inventory amount

Figure 4-10. Amount Indicators

Step Two: Identifying Locations

Introduction

Key Point

Once best locations have been decided, we need a way to identify these locations so that everyone will know what goes where, and how many of each item belong in each location. We have several different strategies for identifying what, where, and how many.

The Signboard Strategy

New Tool

The Signboard Strategy uses signboards to identify what, where, and how many. The three main types of signboards are

- location indicators, which show where items go

- item indicators, which show what specific items go in those places

- amount indicators, which show how many of these items belong there (see Figure 4-10)

Signboards are often used to identify

- names of work areas

- inventory locations

- equipment storage locations

- standard procedures

- machine layout

Photo 4-2. Addresses and Return Addresses on Shelving

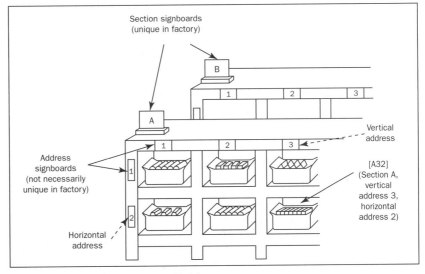

Figure 4-11. Location Indicators on Shelving

Example

For example, in order to identify inventory stored on shelves in a warehouse, a whole system of signboards may be used. Every section of shelving may have a signboard identifying the section. Within that section, vertical and horizontal addresses on shelves can be identified with additional signboards. Each item stored on the shelving may also have a signboard showing the "return address" for that item. The "return address" allows the item to be put back in the proper location once it has been removed (see Photo 4-2 and Figure 4-11).

New Tool

Painting Strategy

The Painting Strategy is a method for identifying locations on floors and walkways. It is called the "Painting Strategy" because paint is the material generally used. However, plastic tape, which can be cut into any length, can also be used. Tape, although more expensive, shows up just as clearly as paint and can be removed if the layout changes.

The Painting Strategy is used to create divider lines that mark off the factory's walking areas ("walkways") from its working areas ("operation areas"). When mapping out walkways and operation areas, we should keep certain factors in mind.

Principles

- U-shaped cell designs are generally more efficient than straight production lines.

- In-process inventory should be positioned carefully for best production flow.

- Floors should be leveled or repaired if possible before divider lines are laid down.

- Walkways should allow for safety and a smooth flow of goods by being wide enough and avoiding twists and turns.

- Divider lines should be between 2 and 4 inches wide.

- Paint colors should be standardized, and the colors should be bright. An example of a color standard is:

  - operation areas are green;
  - walkways are fluorescent orange;
  - divider lines are yellow.

Some types of divider lines include:

- cart storage locations,
- aisle direction (see Photo 4-3),
- door range, to show which way a door swings open (see Photo 4-4),
- place markers for worktables,
- tiger marks, to show areas where inventory and equipment should not be placed, or to show hazardous areas.

Photo 4-3. Aisle Direction Line

Photo 4-4. Door-Range Line

TAKE FIVE

Take five minutes to think about these questions and to jot down your answers.

- Give one example of how you could use the Signboard Strategy to implement Set in Order in your work area.

- Give one example of how you could use the Painting Strategy to implement Set in Order in your work area.

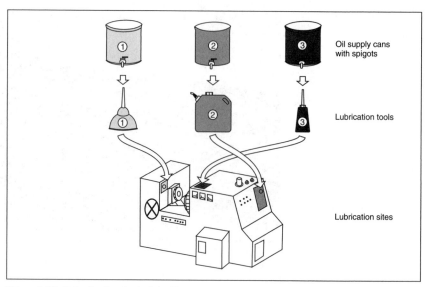

Figure 4-12. Color-Coding for Lubrication

"After" 5S Map

The "after" 5S Map is a kind of signboard. It shows the location of parts, tools, jigs, dies, equipment, and machinery in a given work area after Set in Order has been implemented. Unlike the "before" 5S Map, it should not include arrows showing the flow of work activities. These arrows would make the locations of the items on the map more difficult to read. When posted in the work area, the "after" 5S Map is very effective in communicating the standard for where items are located.

Color-Coding Strategy

Color-coding can be used to show clearly which parts, tools, jigs, and dies are to be used for which purpose. For example, if certain parts are to be used to make a particular product, they can all be color-coded with the same color and even stored in a location that is painted that color. Similarly, if different types of lubricants are to be used on different parts of a machine, the supply containers, oil cans, and machine parts can be color-coded to show what is used where (see Figure 4-12).

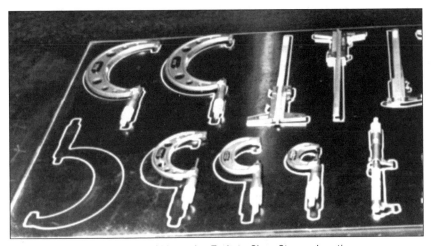

Photo 4-5. Example: Outlining of Measuring Tools to Show Storage Locations

Outlining Strategy

New Tool

Outlining is a good way to show which jigs and tools are stored where. Outlining simply means drawing outlines of jigs and tools in their proper storage positions. When you want to return a tool, the outline provides an additional indication of where it belongs (see Photo 4-5).

TAKE FIVE

Take five minutes to think about these questions and to jot down your answers.

- Give one example of how you could use the Color-Coding Strategy to implement Set in Order in your work area.

- Give one example of how you could use the Outlining Strategy to implement Set in Order in your work area.

In Conclusion

SUMMARY

The second pillar of 5S is Set in Order, which means that items are arranged so that they are easy to find, use, and put back. This is important because it eliminates many types of waste in production and clerical activities.

Standardization means creating a consistent way to carry out tasks and procedures. Another important reason to Set in Order is that orderliness is the core of standardization. The workplace must be orderly before standardization can be implemented effectively. Visual controls are devices used as you Set in Order to communicate the standards for how work should be done. Visual Setting in Order means using visual controls to implement Set in Order activities.

The first step in implementing Set in Order is to decide on appropriate locations. Two sets of principles are helpful in this decision: how to store jigs, tools, and dies; and the principles of motion economy. The principles of motion economy help us to minimize motion waste. While eliminating motion waste it is also important to analyze very carefully why this motion waste has occurred. This analysis can help us to discover methods of manufacturing that approach the zero-waste mark.

The 5S Map is a tool that can be used to evaluate current locations of parts, jigs, tools, equipment, and machinery, and to decide best locations for these items based on the two sets of principles described here.

The second step is to identify best locations once they have been decided. The Signboard and Painting Strategies are both used to identify what should go where and in what quantities. Other tools for identifying best locations are the "after" 5S Map, the Color-Coding Strategy, and the Outlining Strategy.

REFLECTIONS

Now that you've completed this chapter, take five minutes to think about these questions and to jot down your answers.

- What did you learn from reading this chapter that stands out as being particularly useful or interesting?

- Do you have any questions about the topics presented in this chapter? If so, what are they?

- What information do you still need to fully understand the ideas presented?

- How can you get this information?

Chapter 5. The Third Pillar: Shine

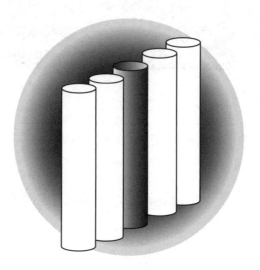

Explanation of the Third Pillar—Shine

BACKGROUND

Introduction

As you've learned in the last two chapters, implementing the five pillars begins when you Sort—getting rid of everything that is not needed in the workplace. This is followed by Setting in Order—putting the remaining needed items into order so that they can easily be found and used by anybody. But what good are Sorting and Setting in Order if the materials we use are dirty and the equipment we depend upon frequently breaks down? This is where the third pillar comes in.

Definition of the Third Pillar

The third pillar is Shine. It is the component that emphasizes the removal of dirt, grime, and dust from the workplace. As such, Shine means that we *keep everything swept and clean.*

Definition

Why Shine Is Important

One of the more obvious purposes of Shine is to turn the workplace into a clean, bright place where everyone will enjoy working. *Another key purpose is to keep everything in top condition so that when someone needs to use something, it is ready to be used.* Companies should abandon the inadequate tradition of annual

Key Point

Figure 5-1. Shine Activities Relieve Stress and Strain

"year-end" or "spring" cleanings. Instead, cleaning should become a deeply ingrained part of daily work habits, so that tools, equipment, and work areas will be ready for use all the time.

Cleanliness for factories and offices is a lot like bathing for human beings (see Figure 5-1). It relieves stress and strain, removes sweat and dirt, and prepares the body and mind for the next day. Both cleanliness and bathing are important for physical and mental health. Just as you would never consider bathing only once a year, performing Shine procedures in a factory should not be an annual activity. By contrast, they should happen on a daily basis.

Figure 5-2. Puddles Cause Slipping and Injury

Problems Avoided by Implementing Shine

Shine activities can play an important part in aiding work efficiency and safety. Cleanliness is also tied in with the morale of employees and their awareness of improvements. Factories that do not implement the Shine pillar suffer the following types of problems:

1. Windows are so dirty that very little sunlight filters through. This leads to poor morale and inefficient work.

2. Defects are less obvious in dark, messy factories.

3. Puddles of oil and water cause slipping and injuries (see Figure 5-2).

4. Machines do not receive sufficient check-up maintenance and tend to break down frequently. This leads to late deliveries.

5. Machines that do not receive sufficient maintenance tend to operate incorrectly at times, which can be hazardous.

6. Cutting shavings can get mixed into production and assembly processes and result in defects.

7. Cutting shavings can blow into people's eyes and create injuries.

8. Filthy work environments can lower morale.

Figure 5-3. Cleaning Means Inspection

Cleaning Means Inspection

Key Point

When we clean an area, it is inevitable that we will also do some inspection of machinery, equipment, and work conditions. Because of this, *cleaning also means inspection* (see Figure 5-3). This is another reason why cleaning is so important. We'll talk more about inspection later in this chapter.

TAKE FIVE

Take five minutes to think about this question and to jot down your answer.

- What are three types of problems in your workplace that could be avoided by implementing Shine procedures?

How to Implement Shine

Planning Your Shine Campaign

Introduction

How-to Steps

Daily cleanliness achieved through Shine activities should be taught as a set of steps and rules that employees learn to maintain with discipline.

Step 1: Determine Shine Targets

Shine targets are grouped in three categories: warehouse items, equipment, and space.

- **Warehouse items** include raw materials, procured subcontracted parts, parts made in-house, assembly components, semifinished and finished products.

- **Equipment** includes machines, welding tools, cutting tools, conveyance tools, general tools, measuring instruments, dies, wheels and casters, worktables, cabinets, desks, chairs, and spare equipment.

- **Space** refers to floors, work areas, walkways, walls, pillars, ceilings, windows, shelves, closets, rooms, and lights.

Step 2: Determine Shine Assignments

Key Point

Workplace cleanliness is the responsibility of everyone who works there. First, we divide the factory into "Shine" areas. Then, we assign specific areas to individuals.

Two tools we can use to do this are:

New Tool

- **A 5S Assignment Map**—One way to communicate Shine assignments is to mark them on a 5S Map. *This 5S Assignment Map shows all of the Shine areas and who is responsible for cleaning them.*

New Tool

- **A 5S Schedule**—*This schedule shows in detail who is responsible for cleaning which areas on which days and times of the day.* The 5S Schedule should be posted in the work area.

Step 3: Determine Shine Methods

Daily Shine activities should include inspection before the shift starts, activities that take place as the work is done, and Shine activities that happen at the end of the shift. It is important to set aside times for these Shine activities so that they eventually become a natural part of the workday.

Figure 5-4. The Five-Minute Shine

Determining Shine methods includes:

New Tool

- **Choosing targets and tools** —Define what will be cleaned in each area and what supplies and equipment will be used.

- **Performing the Five-Minute Shine**—*Cleaning should be practiced daily and should not require a lot of time.* For example, a lot can be accomplished in five minutes of focused cleaning activity. We can assign specific tasks to each block of time devoted to Shine procedures assuming that these tasks will be carried out efficiently (see Figure 5-4).

- **Creating standards for Shine procedures**—People need to know what procedures to follow in order to use their time efficiently. Otherwise, they are likely to spend most of their time getting ready to clean.

Step 4: Prepare Tools

Here we apply Set in Order to our cleaning tools storing them in places where they are easy to find, use, and return.

Step 5: Start to Shine

Here are some suggestions about implementating Shine procedures:

- Be sure to sweep dirt from floor cracks, wall corners, and around pillars.
- Wipe off dust and dirt from walls, windows, and doors.
- Be thorough about cleaning dirt, scraps, oil, dust, rust, cutting shavings, sand, paint, and other foreign matter from all surfaces.
- Use cleansing agents when sweeping is not enough to remove dirt.

Figure 5-5. Systematic Cleaning/Inspection Can Help Prevent Major Equipment Problems

Ongoing Inspection and Maintenance of Cleanliness

The Need for Systematic Cleaning/Inspection

Key Point

As we discussed earlier in this chapter, it is natural to do a certain amount of inspection while implementing Shine activities. *Once daily cleaning and periodic major cleanups become a habit, we can start incorporating systematic inspection procedures into our Shine procedures.* This turns "cleaning" into "cleaning/inspection."

Even when equipment in the workplace appears to function normally, it may be developing many problems (see Figure 5-5). Generally, when machines or other equipment begin to show signs of minor, sporadic malfunctions, the operators—not the maintenance people—notice it first. It is important to take advantage of operator sensitivity toward equipment.

The following types of equipment problems frequently exist in factories:

1. Oil leaks from the equipment onto the floor.
2. Machines are so dirty that operators avoid touching them.
3. Gauge displays and other indicators are too dirty to be read.
4. Nuts and bolts are either loose or missing.
5. Motors overheat.
6. Sparks flare from power cords.
7. V-belts are loose or broken.
8. Some machines make strange noises.

Daily cleaning/inspection can help locate and correct these problems.

Steps in Cleaning/Inspection

The steps in cleaning/inspection parallel the steps in the Shine procedures, but place greater emphasis on the maintenance of machines and equipment. These cleaning/inspection steps are listed below.

Step 1. Determine Cleaning/Inspection Targets

The targets for cleaning/inspection are basically the same as the equipment-related targets noted earlier with regard to Shine duties. These include machines, equipment, jigs, dies, cutting tools, and measuring instruments.

Step 2. Assign Cleanliness/Inspection Jobs

In principle, the people who carry out cleaning/inspection on a particular machine should be the same people who operate the machine. Often one person operates several machines (as in multi-process handling). In this case, it is a good idea also to involve line supervisors and group leaders in cleaning/inspection duties.

Once cleaning/inspection job assignments are determined, they should be written up (1) on a large signboard for the workshop or (2) on small signs attached to each target machine.

TAKE FIVE

Take five minutes to think about these questions and to jot down your answers.

- What types of procedures and schedules does your company currently use to clean and inspect its equipment? Who does the cleaning and inspection?

- What are some ways that your company could involve shopfloor workers more in cleaning and inspecting equipment?

Mechanism	No.	Point	Clean	Lubricate	Replace	Restore
Lubrication system	26.	Is there any dirt or dust in the oil inlets?	O			
	27.	Do the oil level indicators show adequate levels?		O		
1. Oil inlets	28.	Can the oil level indicators be clearly seen?	O			
	29.	Are there any cracks in the oil tank?				O
2. Tank	30.	Is the bottom of the oil tank dirty?	O			
	31.	Is the oil in the tank dirty?			O	
	32.	Is there any oil leakage from the tank or pipe joints?			O	O
3. Oil pipes	33.	Are oil levels adequate?		O		
	34.	Is the correct type of oil being used?			O	
4. Lubrication sites	35.	Is there any clogging in the oil pipes?			O	O
	36.	Is there any dust or dirt at lubrication sites?	O			
	37.	Are the lubrication tools dirty?	O			

Table 5-1. Part of a Cleaning/Inspection Checklist

Step 3. Determine Clean/Inspection Methods

New Tool

Once Cleaning/Inspection targets and job assignments have been determined, it is time to examine methods. *First, list all of the inspection check items and combine them to make a "Cleaning/ Inspection Checklist."* Table 5-1 shows an example of part of a Cleaning/Inspection Checklist.

Step 4. Implement Cleaning/Inspection

Key Point

When actually implementing cleaning/inspection, the key is to use all your senses to detect abnormalities. Inspection is not simply a visual activity. Here are some tips to diagnose abnormalities:

- Look closely at how the machine works and watch for slight defects (e.g., oil leakage, debris scattering, deformation, wear, warping, mold, missing items, lopsidedness, inclinations, color changes).

- Listen closely for changes in the sounds the machine makes while operating (e.g., sporadic sounds, odd sounds).

- Use your nose to detect burning smells or other unusual odors (e.g., burning rubber, cleansing agents).

- Touch the machine where it is safe during operation and during downtime to detect deviations from normal conditions (e.g., strange vibrations, wobbling, looseness, excessive heat, shifting).

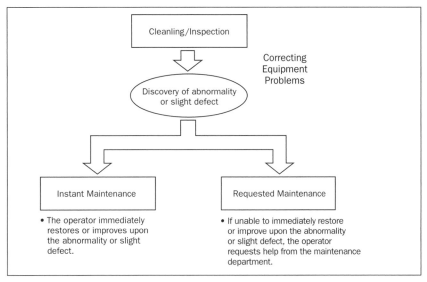

Figure 5-6. Two Approaches for Correcting Equipment Problems

Step 5. Correct Equipment Problems

Key Point

All equipment abnormalities or slight defects should be fixed or improved. There are two approaches to these repairs (see Figure 5-6).

Instant Maintenance

Whenever possible, an operator should immediately fix or improve a problem he or she discovers during cleaning/inspection. This "instant maintenance" requires that operators know what level of maintenance work they can handle by themselves and immediately.

Requested Maintenance

In some cases, an operator may determine that a defect or problem is too difficult to handle alone or immediately. In this situation, the operator should attach a maintenance card to the site of the problem in order to flag the problem and make it visible. He or she should also issue a maintenance kanban to request help from the maintenance department.

New Tool

It is also a good idea to log requested maintenance items onto a Checklist of Needed Maintenance Activities. Once a requested maintenance item has been taken care of and its result confirmed, the item should be checked off in the "confirmation" column of the checklist. The maintenance card should then be retrieved from the machine where it is attached.

In Conclusion

SUMMARY

The third pillar is Shine. These activities keep everything swept and clean. One of the key purposes of cleaning is to keep all equipment in top condition so that it is always ready to be used. When the third pillar is not well implemented, the problems that arise include: poor employee morale, safety hazards, equipment breakdowns, and an increased number of product defects.

There are five steps in implementing Shine in your workplace. These are: (1) Determine Shine targets; (2) Determine Shine assignments; (3) Determine Shine methods; (4) Prepare Shine tools; and (5) Implement Shine. It is important to note that workplace cleanliness is the responsibility of everyone who works there. Two of the tools used in the implementation of Shine are 5S Schedules and the Five-Minute Shine.

Once daily cleaning and periodic major cleanups are a habit, systematic inspection can be incorporated into the Shine procedures. This turns "cleaning" into "cleaning/ inspection." The steps of this inspection parallel the steps of the Shine procedure, but they place greater emphasis on the maintenance of machines and equipment. These steps are: (1) Determine cleaning/inspection targets; (2) Assign cleaning/inspection jobs; (3) Determine cleaning/inspection methods; (4) Implement cleaning/inspection, using all your senses to detect abnormalities; and (5) Correct equipment problems by repairing all defects immediately or making a formal request to the maintenance team to schedule the repair. Two of the tools used in implementing cleaning/ inspection are Cleaning/Inspection Checklists and Checklists of Needed Maintenance Activities.

REFLECTIONS

Now that you've completed this chapter, take five minutes to think about these questions and to jot down your answers.

- What did you learn from reading this chapter that stands out as being particularly useful or interesting?

- Do you have any questions about the topics presented in this chapter? If so, what are they?

- What information do you still need to fully understand the ideas presented?

- How can you get this information?

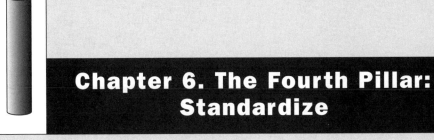

Chapter 6. The Fourth Pillar: Standardize

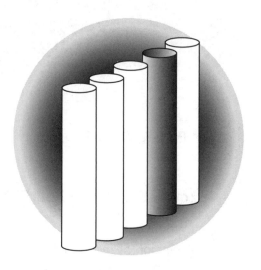

Explanation of the Fourth Pillar— Standardize

OVER **VIEW**

Introduction

In Chapters 3, 4, and 5 you learned about Sort, Set in Order, and Shine. In this chapter you will learn about a way to make sure the first three pillars are always implemented.

Definition of the Fourth Pillar

Definition

Standardize, the fourth pillar of our visual workplace, differs from Sort, Set in Order, and Shine. This is because it is the method you use to maintain the first three pillars. In Chapter 4 we defined standardization as creating a consistent way that tasks and procedures are done. Building on this definition, *we may define Standardize as the result that exists when the first three pillars— Sort, Set in Order, and Shine—are properly maintained.*

Why Standardize Is Important

Example

When you think about a city you might say that a well-kept city block is one that has been swept and washed clean of debris and dirt. In the 5S context, a well-kept city block would be one in which the results of Sort, Set in Order, and Shine are maintained. This means that it would include only buildings, plantings, streets, and utilities that add to the beauty or function of the area, that these items are well laid out, and that the area is well maintained.

By contrast, a poorly kept city block might include broken-down or unused buildings, have no plantings, have inadequate utilities, and be dirty and unsightly.

In other words, Standardize integrates Sort, Set in Order, and Shine into a unified whole. After all, what good is the implementation of the first three pillars if conditions constantly deteriorate to what they were before implementation?

Problems Avoided by Implementing Standardize Activities

Here are some of the problems that result when we do not implement Standardize well.

- Conditions go back to their old undesirable levels even after a companywide 5S implementation campaign.

- At the end of the day, piles of unneeded items are left from the day's production and lie scattered around the production equipment.

- Tool storage sites become disorganized and must be put back in order at the end of the day.

- Cutting shavings constantly fall on the floor and must be swept up.

- Even after implementing Sort and Set in Order, it does not take long for office workers to start accumulating more stationery supplies than they need.

Key Point

These problems and others reveal backsliding in gains made from implementing Sort, Set in Order, and Shine Activities. *The basic purpose of the Standardize pillar is to prevent setbacks in the first three pillars, to make implementing them a daily habit, and to make sure that all three pillars are maintained in their fully implemented state.*

How to Implement Standardize

Making Sort, Set in Order, and Shine a Habit

Introduction

The three steps to making Sort, Set in Order, and Shine activities (the three pillars or 3S) a habit are

- Step 1: Decide who is responsible for which activities with regard to maintaining 3S conditions.

- Step 2: To prevent backsliding, integrate 3S maintenance duties into regular work activities.

- Step 3: Check on how well 3S conditions are being maintained.

We will discuss each of these in greater detail in the next section of this chapter. As you read this section, you will notice that some of the tools for implementing Standardize (such as the 5S Map) are familiar to you from your study of the Sort, Set in Order, and Shine pillars. This is because in order to standardize we must use these same tools in a more systematic way to make sure that the first three pillars are maintained.

1. Assign 3S Responsibilities

Key Point

When it comes to maintaining three pillar conditions, everyone must know exactly what they are responsible for doing and exactly when, where, and how to do it. If people are not given clear 3S job assignments based on their own workplaces, the Sort, Set in Order, and Shine activities will not have much meaning.

Similarly, clear 3S instructions must be given to the people who deliver goods from outside suppliers. The delivery sites should be clearly marked and a 5S Map posted to show where each supplier's goods are to be unloaded. At each unloading site, signboards should make it clear whose things go where and in what amount. The suppliers should be made responsible for maintaining 3S conditions at their own unloading sites and encouraged to join in full 5S implementation.

5S Job Cycle Chart		Div./Dept./ Section	Production Div. 1, Assembly Dept. A			
		Entered by:	Comarella	Date:	1 Feb 1994	

No.	5S Job	Sort	Set in Order	Shine	Standardize	Sustain	A	B	C	D	E	F
1.	Red-tag strategy (occasional, companywide)	O									O	
2.	Red-tag strategy (repeated)	O				O						
3.	Place indicators (check or make)		O						O			
4.	Item indicators (check or make)		O						O			
5.	Amount indicators (check or make)		O						O			
6.	Sweep around line			O					O			
7.	Sweep within line			O					O			
8.	Sweep around worktable			O					O			
9.	Sweep on and under worktable			O					O			
10.	Sweep work areas and walkways											

Figure 6-1. A 5S Job Cycle Chart

Tools for assigning 3S responsibilities include:

- 5S Maps (See Chapter 4, pages 56-57)

- 5S Schedules (See Chapter 5, page 72)

- *5S Job Cycle Charts, which list the 5S jobs to be done in each area, and set a frequency cycle for each job* (see Figure 6-1).

New Tool

In the example shown in Figure 6-1, 5S duties are sorted out according to the first three pillars and the scheduling cycle. In the figure, code letters are used for the various cycle periods: A is for "continuously," B for "daily (mornings)," C for "daily (evenings)," D for "weekly," E for "monthly," and F for "occasionally." Each 5S job assignee can then use these charts as 5S Checklists. This particular example shows clearly who is responsible for each job, which area, what to do, and when to do it.

2. Integrate 3S Duties into Regular Work Duties

Key Point

If people carry out three pillar maintenance duties only when they see three pillar conditions slipping, then five pillar implementation has not yet taken root. Maintenance must become a natural part of everyone's regular work duties. *In other words, the five pillars—centered on maintaining 3S conditions— must be part of the normal work flow.* We sometimes refer to this as "5S line integration" or establishing a five pillar flow.

Visual 5S and Five-Minute 5S are two approaches that help make 5S maintenance work part of the everyday work routine.

Visual 5S

New Tool

The Visual 5S approach makes the level of five pillar conditions obvious at a glance. This is particularly helpful in factories that handle a great variety and number of materials.

The main point of Visual 5S is that anyone should be able to distinguish between abnormal and normal conditions at a glance.

In Chapter 4 we defined visual controls as devices that tell us at a glance how work should be done. Clearly, the use of visual controls is central to the successful implementation of Visual 5S.

Example

As a factory example, consider a drill-press process where Set in Order has been applied so that the position and amount of each finished workpiece is clearly indicated. As an additional visual aid, the place where the last batch item goes can be marked with a thick red line to indicate that it is time to stop and send the batch to the next process (see Figure 6-2).

Five-Minute 5S

New Tool

In Chapter 5 you learned about the Five-Minute Shine technique. Five-Minute 5S is similar, but it covers all five pillars rather than just the third. When using the Visual 5S approach, instant visibility can act as a trigger for taking immediate three pillar action (Sort, Set in Order, and Shine activities) against the discovered abnormalities (i.e., overproduction, disorder, and contamination).

We must also deal with the question of how skillfully and efficiently these actions are carried out. Instead of allowing two

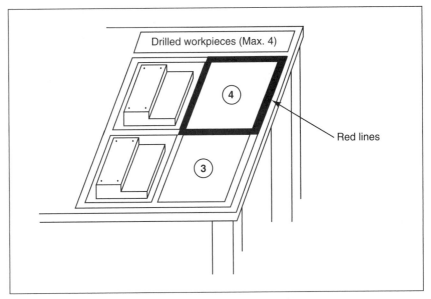

Figure 6-2. Visual 5S Method for Indicating Maximum Batch Size

hours for removing all of the cutting shavings from the floor, we can set up a half-hour or a one-hour Shine procedure that accomplishes the same task. The term "Five-Minute 5S" is a loose one—the actual time can be three minutes, six minutes, or whatever is appropriate. *The point is to make the five pillar work brief, efficient, and habitual.* Figure 6-3 shows a signboard that was made as part of a Five-Minute 5S campaign.

Key Point

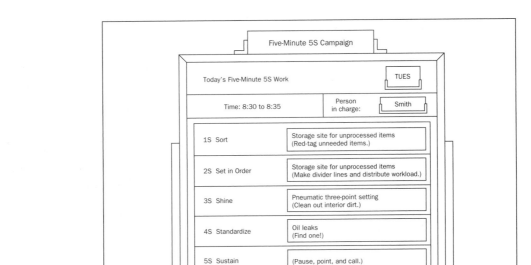

Figure 6-3. Five-minute 5S Signboard

	Standardization-Level Checklist	Dept.: Assembly Dept. 1	Feb. 15, 1994		
		Assigned area	Entered by: McCarthy	Page	1/1

No.	Process and checkpoint	Sort	Set in Order	Shine	Total	Previous total
1.	Work at Line A, Process 1	1 2 3 (4) 5	1 (2) 3 4 5	1 (2) 3 4 5	8	6
2.	"	1 (2) 3 4 5	1 2 (3) 4 5	1 2 (3) 4 5	8	6
3.	"	1 (2) 3 4 5	1 (2) 3 4 5	1 (2) 3 4 5	6	5
4.	"	1 (2) 3 4 5	1 2 (3) 4 5	1 (2) 3 4 5	7	7
5.	"	1 2 (3) 4 5	1 2 (3) 4 5	1 2 3 (4) 5	10	6
6.	"	1 2 3 (4) 5	1 2 3 (4) 5	1 2 3 (4) 5	12	8
7.	Average and total for Line A	1 2 (2.6) 3 4 5	1 2 (2.8) 3 4 5	1 2 (2.8) 3 4 5	(50)	(38)

Figure 6-4. Standardization-Level Checklist

3. Check on 3S Maintenance Level

After we have assigned three pillar jobs and have incorporated three pillar (or five pillar) maintenance into the everyday work routine, we need to evaluate how well the three pillars are being maintained.

For this, we can use a Standardization-level Checklist. To evaluate the effectiveness of the maintenance activities, the evaluator ranks the Sort, Set in Order, and Shine levels on a scale of 1 to 5. Such checklists can be made for specific workshops and/or production processes. One example is shown in Figure 6-4.

5S Checklists like the one in Figure 6-5 are used to check five pillar levels in the factory as a whole. When a company implements a 5S Month of intensive activities, 5S Checklists should be used to make weekly evaluations of five pillar conditions.

New Tool

New Tool

Factory: Tokai plant		5S Checklist (for factories)		Scoring:	3 = Very good			

				2 = Good
				1 = OK
Checked by: NK				0 = Not good

| Location | Check Item | Check Description | Year and month: | | | | | |
			1	2	3	4	5	T
Outdoors (overall)	Are storage areas clearly determined?	Areas for paring, pallets, temporary materials storage, delivered goods reception, trash processing, and boxes	0	2	0	2	0	4
	Have paths been clearly defined?	Have white and yellow lines been laid down?	0	2	0	2	0	4
		Are traffic signs used?	0	3	0	3	0	6
		Are there any exposed wires or pipes?	1	3	1	3	1	9
	Are outdoor areas kept clean?	Are ashtrays, trash cans, gardens, entrance areas, windows, and paths kept clean?	1	3	1	3	1	9
	Are there any unneeded items?	Are signboards, copy machines, and pathways arranged properly?	1	1	1	1	1	5
Clerical (overall)	Have temp storage areas been clearly defined?	Have fire-extinguishing equipment and emergency exits been established?	2	3	2			
	Are office areas kept clean?	Are the walls dirty?						

Figure 6-5. 5S Checklist for an Entire Factory

TAKE FIVE

Take five minutes to think about these questions and to jot down your answers.

- Identify one way that Visual 5S could be used in your work area to help distinguish between normal and abnormal work conditions at a glance.

- Identify one Five-Minute 5S activity you could do daily that would improve the efficiency of your work.

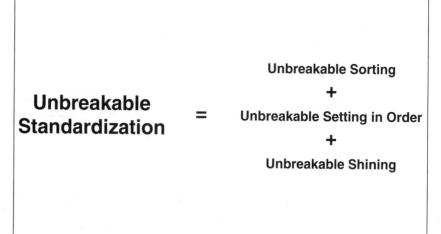

Figure 6-6. Defining Unbreakable Standardization

Taking It to the Next Level: Prevention

The Concept of Prevention

When we find that tools have not been put back correctly, we immediately take care of them. When we find an oil puddle on the floor, we immediately mop it up. Making these actions habitual is the foundation of Standardize. *However, when the same problems keep happening over and over again, it is time to take the concept of Standardize to the next level: prevention.*

To take this pillar to a higher level, we must ask "why?" Why do unneeded items accumulate (despite Sort procedures)? Why do tools get put back incorrectly (despite Set in Order procedures)? Why do floors get dirty (despite Shine procedures)? When we ask "why" repeatedly, we eventually find the source of the problem and can address that source with a fundamental improvement. Such improvements can help us develop *Unbreakable Standardization* (see Figure 6–6), which means:

- *unbreakable Sorting*

- *unbreakable Setting in Order*

- *unbreakable Shining*

Prevent Unneeded Items from Accumulating (Preventive Sort Procedures)

The Red-Tag Strategy described in Chapter 3 is our main means of sorting out unneeded items. This strategy is a visual control method that enables anyone to see at a glance which items are no longer needed. However, we should note that the Red-Tag Strategy is an after-the-fact approach that deals with unneeded items that have accumulated. No matter how often we implement this strategy, unneeded items will accumulate in the interim.

Definition

Nowadays, smart companies are shifting from this type of "after-the-fact" sorting to preventive sorting. *Preventive sorting means that instead of waiting until unneeded items accumulate, we find ways to prevent their accumulation.* We could also call this approach "unbreakable" sorting because once sort procedures have been implemented, having only needed items in the workplace becomes an "unbreakable" condition.

Key Point

To achieve unbreakable sorting, we must prevent unneeded items from even entering the workplace. These words—"only what is needed"—have a familiar ring to anyone acquainted with the just-in-time (JIT) philosophy and program. To prevent the accumulation of unneeded inventory, we must find a way to procure and produce only those materials that are needed, only when they are needed, and only in the amount needed.

For example, suppose your company is scheduled to produce a certain number of units of a product during a particular month. Ideally, at the beginning of this month, only the parts needed to produce the scheduled number of units would be delivered to you from your suppliers. For any given part, your company might even receive the part in several deliveries, depending on the type of part and the delivery considerations.

Receiving parts just-in-time for production rather than storing large quantities of parts in advance eliminates many of the potential costs associated with maintaining inventory. As well, receiving parts just-in-time is a preventive measure that avoids the accumulation of parts that need to be sorted.

Prevent Things from Having to Be Put Back (Preventive Set in Order Procedures)

Definition

Key Point

Preventive setting in order means keeping Set in Order procedures from breaking down. To achieve preventive setting in order, we must somehow prevent the inefficiency that results from the lack of orderly control of any specific item. There are two ways to do this: (1) make it difficult to put things in the wrong place and (2) make it impossible to put things in the wrong place.

The first method relies heavily on discipline and visual controls. Clearly marked storage sites show at a glance what goes where and in what amount. When it is obvious what goes where and in what amount, it is also obvious when things are not put back properly. As people practice returning things, such visual setting in order becomes habitual. This condition supports setting in order that is difficult to break.

However, there is still a big difference between setting in order that is difficult to break and setting in order that is unbreakable. Why settle for the first when the second is possible? But how do we achieve unbreakable setting in order?

The 5 Whys and 1 How (5W1H) Approach

We begin by asking "why?" until we identify the underlying causes— for every answer we get we must ask "why" again. *Usually we ask "why" at least five times to get to the root of the problem. When we do find the underlying cause, we ask "how" we can fix it. Accordingly, this method is called the "5W1H" approach.*

New Tool

Key Point

When we ask "why" setting in order is breakable, we find that one answer is because people make mistakes putting things back. At this point, we need to identify what types of items are not being returned correctly. Once we identify this, the question is how to achieve unbreakable setting in order by making it impossible to return them to the wrong place. *If we can somehow eliminate the need to return items at all, we can achieve unbreakable setting in order.* Three techniques for doing this are: suspension, incorporation, and use elimination.

Photo 6–1. Tools suspended from an overhead rack

Suspension

New Tool

In the Suspension technique, tools are literally suspended from above, just within reach of the user. Photo 6-1 shows this method in practice. Here a weighted pulley device is used to suspend tools from an overhead rack. When the operator finishes using the tool, he merely releases it and it automatically returns to its proper storage place.

While this techniques does not eliminate the need to return items to a specific place, it does effectively eliminate the need for people to return them. People may make mistakes in returning things, but suspension devices do not. This technique achieves unbreakable Setting in Order.

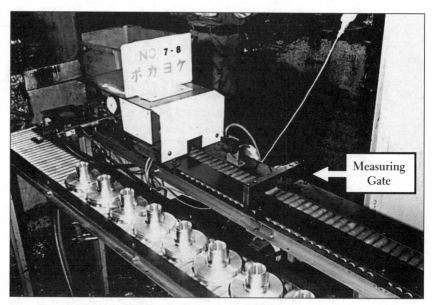

Photo 6-2. Incorporating a Measuring Gate into the Process Flow

New Tool

Incorporation

Incorporation means creating a flow of goods or operations in a factory process in which (1) jigs, tools, and measuring instruments are smoothly integrated into the process and (2) such devices are stored where they are used and therefore do not have to be returned after use.

Photo 6-2 shows an example where a measuring gate has been incorporated into a cutting process for an automobile part. The measuring gate catches any pieces that have not been machined to the correct height. This measuring procedure is an example of "mistake-proofing" (or poka-yoke). The incorporation of the measuring gate into the cutting process means that its storage place is also its place of use. It is therefore used (for full-lot inspection) without having to be put back anywhere.

New Tool

Key Point

Use Elimination

Suspending or incorporating jigs, tools, or measuring instruments effectively eliminates the need to return them after each use. However, these items are still being used.

The question is whether there is some way to serve the function of the tool without using the jig, tool, or measuring instrument. A Set in Order approach that eliminates the use of a particular jig, tool, or measuring instrument is in fact unbreakable setting in order.

There are three techniques for eliminating the use of certain tools:

Tool unification

Definition

Tool unification means combining the functions of two or more tools into a single tool. It is an approach that usually reaches back to the design stage. For example, we can reduce the variety of die designs to unify dies, or make all fasteners that require a screwdriver conform to the same kind of screwdriver, flat-tip or Phillips.

Tool substitution

Definition

Tool substitution means using something other than a tool to serve the tool's function, thereby eliminating the tool. For example, it is sometimes possible to replace wrench-turned bolts with hand-turned butterfly-grip bolts, thereby eliminating the need for a wrench.

Method substitution

If we substitute ordinary wrench-turned bolts with hand-turned butterfly-grip bolts, we have eliminated the wrench, but we have not eliminated the method (bolt fastening).

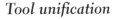

Definition

Bolt fastening is just one way to fasten things. Fastening pins, clamps, and cylinders can also be used for this purpose. *We may find we can improve efficiency even more by replacing one method with another. This is "method substitution."*

TAKE FIVE

Take five minutes to think about these questions and to jot down your answers.

- Give one example each of how suspension, incorporation, and use elimination could make it unnecessary to return specific items in your work area

- Give one example of how you could prevent unneeded items from accumulating in your work area.

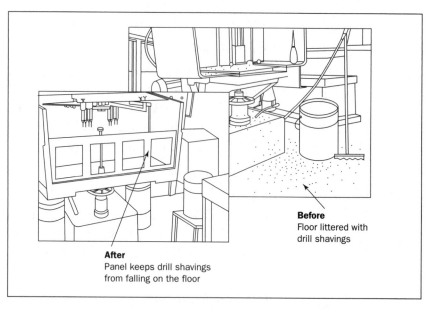

Before
Floor littered with
drill shavings

After
Panel keeps drill shavings
from falling on the floor

Figure 6-7. A Preventive Cleanliness Device for a Drill Press

Prevent Things from Getting Dirty (Preventive Shine Procedures)

Definition

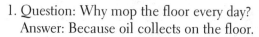

Key Point

X

Example

Preventive Shine Procedures will prevent things from getting dirty to begin with. Anyone who has participated in 5S implementation can tell you that the initial cleanup is very hard work. *To minimize the drudgery of cleaning up, the key is to treat contamination problems at their source.* The 5 Why approach can be applied to figure out why dirt is being generated, and how this problem can be fixed. For example, instead of mopping up oil puddles, figure out where the oil is leaking from and repair the leak.

1. Question: Why mop the floor every day?
   Answer: Because oil collects on the floor.

2. Question: Why does oil collect on the floor every day?
   Answer: Because there's a leak from the drill press machine.

3. Question: Why is there a leak from the drill press machine?
   Answer: Because oil is leaking from a valve.

4. Question: Why is oil leaking from a valve?
   Answer: Because it's broken.

5. Question: Why hasn't the valve been replaced?
   Answer: Because we didn't notice it was broken.

6. Question: How can we coordinate getting the valve fixed?
   Answer: The maintenance team will order the part and the operator will replace it.

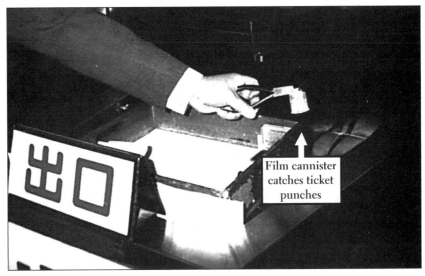

Photo 6-3. Ticket Punch Equipped with a Device to Prevent Debris

Examples

Key Point

In Figure 6-7, we see how a side panel has been added to a drill press to prevent drill shavings from scattering close to its source (the drill bit), thereby eliminating the need to sweep up shavings. This is the key when installing such preventive devices: *The closer you can get to the source of the contamination, the better you will be able to standardize procedures.*

Photo 6-3 shows an improvement made in a railway ticket booth. Previously, booths where ticket punchers worked had to be swept out every two or three hours due to the steady accumulation of punched ticket pieces on the floors. Now, instead of allowing debris to drop to the floor, the punches incorporate empty plastic film containers to catch the ticket pieces. This improvement effectively eliminated the need for frequent floor sweeping and is an example of a preventive Shine measure.

TAKE FIVE

Take five minutes to think about this question and to jot down your answer.

- Give one example of how the 5 Why technique could help identify the cause of a cleanliness problem in your work area.

97

In Conclusion

SUMMARY

The fourth pillar is Standardize, which is the result of properly maintaining the first three pillars—Sort, Set in Order, and Shine. The basic purpose of Standardize is to prevent setbacks in the first three pillars, to make them a daily habit, and to make sure they are maintained in their fully implemented state.

The first part of implementing the fourth pillar involves making Sort, Set in Order, and Shine a habit. The three steps in this process are (1) Assigning three pillar job responsibilities; (2) Integrating three pillar duties into regular work duties; and (3) Checking on the maintenance of the three pillars. When it comes to maintaining three pillar conditions, everyone must know exactly what they are responsible for doing and exactly when, where, and how to do it. The five pillars must become part of the normal work flow. And 5S work must be brief, efficient, and habitual. Some of the tools used in making Sort, Set in Order, and Shine procedures a habit are: 5S Job Cycle Charts, Visual 5S, Five-Minute 5S, a Standardization Level Checklist, and 5S Checklists for Factories.

The second part of implementing the fourth pillar involves taking Standardize to the next level: prevention. Unbreakable standardization means making Sort, Set in Order, and Shine procedures unbreakable. The three aspects of unbreakable standardization are preventive Sort procedures, preventive Set in Order procedures, and preventive Shine procedures.

Preventive sorting means that instead of waiting until unneeded items accumulate we find ways to prevent their accumulation. To do this, we must prevent unneeded items from even entering the workplace. Preventive setting in order means keeping the Set in Order procedures from breaking down. We do this by making it difficult or impossible to put things back in the wrong place. Several techniques for accomplishing this are: the 5 Whys and 1 How Approach (5W1H), Suspension, Incorporation, and Use Elimination. Finally, preventive shining means preventing things from getting dirty. The key to preventive shining is treating contamination problems at their source. The closer you can get to the source of contamination, the better you will be able to implement preventive shining.

REFLECTIONS

- What did you learn from reading this chapter that stands out as being particularly useful or interesting?

- Do you have any questions about the topics presented in this chapter? If so, what are they?

- What information do you still need to fully understand the ideas presented?

- How can you get this information?

Chapter 7. The Fifth Pillar: Sustain

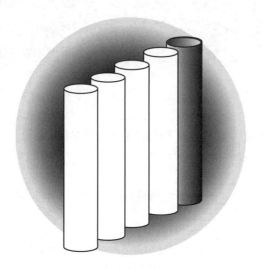

Explanation of the Fifth Pillar—Sustain

Introduction

In Chapters 3 through 5 you learned the tools and techniques of the Sort, Set in Order, and Shine pillars. In Chapter 6 you learned how to standardize the implementation of these three pillars. But what good are standards and procedures without the discipline to follow them? This is where the fifth pillar comes in.

Definition of the Fifth Pillar

Definition

The fifth pillar is Sustain. In the context of the five pillars, to Sustain means to make a habit of properly maintaining correct procedures.

In your life in general, what do you mean when you talk about sustaining something? Usually, you think of it as drawing on something from inside yourself in order to maintain a course of action—even when forces in your life challenge this effort.

Photo 7-1. A Disorderly Workplace

Problems Avoided by Implementing Sustain

Here are some of the things that happen in a company when commitment to the five pillars is not sustained.

1. Unneeded items begin piling up as soon as sorting is completed (see Photo 7-1).

2. No matter how well Set in Order is planned and implemented, tools and jigs do not get returned to their designated places after use.

3. No matter how dirty equipment becomes, little or nothing is done to clean it.

4. Items are left protruding into walkways, causing people to trip and get injured.

5. Dirty machines start to malfunction and produce defective goods.

6. Dark, dirty, disorganized workplaces lower workers' morale.

These 5S related problems and others are likely to occur in any factory or office that lacks a commitment to Sustain the five pillar gains over time.

Figure 7-1. Contemplating the Rewards of Sustaining Behavior

Why Sustain Is Important

Key Point

Example

Usually you commit yourself to sustain a particular course of action because the rewards for keeping to the course of action are greater than the rewards for departing from it (see Figure 7-1). Viewed another way, the consequences of not keeping to the course of action may be greater than the consequences of keeping to it.

For example, suppose you want to start an exercise program—say you decide you want to work out at a gym three times a week. You probably have difficulty sustaining this course of action. This is because forces in your life, such as limits on your time and energy as well as the power of inertia, challenge this plan. However, if the rewards of sticking to your exercise program (for example, feeling and looking better) are greater than the rewards of not sticking to it (for example, having more time for other things that you need to do), your commitment will increase and you will probably sustain this program over time.

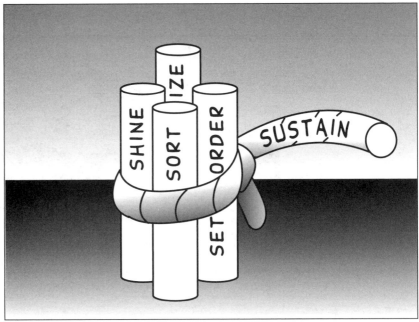

Figure 7-2. The Sustain Pillar Holds the First Four Pillars Together

Key Point

The same principle applies in your 5S implementation. Without your commitment to Sustain the benefits of the 5S activities, implementation of the first four pillars quickly falls apart (see Figure 7-2). However, if the rewards of implementing the first four pillars are greater for you than the rewards of not implementing them, sustaining them through the fifth pillar should be something you take to naturally.

So, what are the rewards for you of implementing the first four pillars? You've probably discovered them for yourself at this point. Implementation of the first four pillars should make your workplace more pleasant to work in, your job more satisfying, and communication with your coworkers easier. It should also make your work more efficient and of better quality, which will hopefully lead to reward of your efforts by your company.

It's true that the five pillars take time to implement, but this investment of time will bring a great return, for both you and your company.

Figure 7-3. Creating the Conditions to Sustain Your Fitness Plan

How to Implement Sustain

Creating Conditions to Sustain Your Plans

OVER VIEW

The implementation of the Sustain pillar is different from that of the Sort, Set in Order, Shine, or Standardize pillars in the sense that the results are not visible and cannot be measured. Commitment to it exists in people's hearts and minds and only their behavior shows its presence. Because of this it cannot exactly be "implemented" like a technique. However, we can create conditions that encourage the implementation of the Sustain pillar.

Example

For instance, going back to our exercise program example, how could you create conditions in your own life that would encourage sustaining your plan to work out at a gym three times a week? You might:

- Join a gym with a friend so you can work out together and encourage each other (see Figure 7-3).

- Create a workout schedule with your friend.

- Make a plan with your spouse to eat dinner later three nights a week so you can go to the gym after work.

- Get extra sleep on the nights before you work out, so that you won't be too tired by the end of the day to follow through with your exercise plan.

These conditions would make it easier for you to sustain your schedule of exercising at the gym three times a week.

Similarly, you and your company can create conditions or structures that will help Sustain a commitment to the five pillars. The types of conditions that are most useful for this are:

- **Awareness.** You and your coworkers need to understand what the five pillars are and how important it is to Sustain them.

- **Time.** You need to have or make enough time in your work schedule to perform 5S implementation.

- **Structure**. You need to have a structure for how and when 5S activities will be implemented.

- **Support.** You need to have support for your efforts from management, in terms of acknowledgement, leadership, and resources.

- **Rewards and Recognition.** Your efforts need to be rewarded.

- **Satisfaction and Excitement.** The implementation of the five pillars needs to be fun and satisfying for you and the company. This excitement and satisfaction gets communicated from person to person, allowing 5S implementation to build as it involves more people.

TAKE FIVE

Take five minutes to think about this question and to jot down your answer.

- What are some conditions that would help sustain people's commitment to 5S implementation in your workplace?

Roles In Implementation

In order to Sustain 5S implementation in your company, both you and the company management have important roles to play. Part of this role involves creating the conditions that Sustain 5S activities. The other part involves demonstrating a commitment to 5S yourself.

The Role of Management

The supervisors and managers in your company have a major role to play in ensuring the success of the five pillars by creating conditions that help sustain 5S activities. This role includes:

- educating you and your coworkers about 5S concepts, tools, and techniques;

- creating teams for implementation

- allowing time for implementation and creating schedules for this work

- providing resources for 5S implementation, such as supplies

- acknowledging and supporting 5S efforts

- encouraging creative involvement by all workers, listening to their ideas, and acting on them

- creating both tangible and intangible rewards for 5S efforts

- promoting ongoing 5S efforts

Your supervisors and managers also have an important role to play in implementing the fifth pillar in their own work. When they Sustain the first four pillars, they perform three very important functions.

- improving the quality and efficiency of their own work

- teaching by example

- demonstrating the company's commitment to 5S implementation

Figure 7-4. Enthusiasm for 5S Implementation

Your Role

Similarly, you have an important role to play in creating the conditions that Sustain 5S activities. This role includes:

- continuing to learn more about 5S implementation
- helping to educate your coworkers about the 5S
- being enthusiastic about 5S implementation
- helping to promote 5S implementation efforts

You also have an important role to play in order to Sustain 5S activities in your own work. This role includes:

- taking the initiative to figure out ways to implement the five pillars in your work on a daily basis
- asking your supervisor or manager for the support or resources you need to implement the five pillars
- participating fully in company 5S implementation efforts
- bringing to your supervisor or manager your creative ideas for promoting or implementing the five pillars
- participating fully in company 5S promotion efforts (see Figure 7-4)

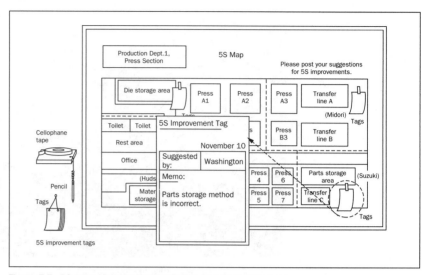

Figure 7-5. 5S Map Used to Gather Improvement Suggestions

Tools and Techniques to Sustain 5S Implementation

There are many tools and techniques your company can use to help sustain commitment to 5S implementation. We offer these below so you will be aware of them. At some point in your 5S implementation work, you may be called upon to use or even coordinate the use of these techniques.

5S Slogans

5S Slogans communicate the themes of the five pillar campaign in your company. They are most effective when they are suggested by you and your coworkers. They can be displayed on buttons, stickers, flags, or posters.

5S Posters

Posters displaying 5S Slogans or descriptions of 5S activities can be posted throughout the workplace. They can serve to remind everyone of the importance of the five pillars,or to communicate the results or status of 5S activities.

5S Photo Exhibits and Storyboards

When it comes to communication about 5S implementation, the old saying that a "picture is worth a thousand words" is definitely true. *Photo Exhibits and Storyboards showing the before and after of 5S implementation activities are powerful tools for promoting the five pillars. Photos and Storyboards can also communicate the status of five pillar activities.*

New Tools

5S Newsletters

5S Newsletters are in-house news bulletins centered on five pillar topics. They carry factory reports on 5S conditions and activities. 5S Newsletters are most effective when issued on a regular basis, perhaps once or twice a month and at staff meetings.

5S Maps

5S Maps can also be used to get employees involved in five pillar improvement on an ongoing basis (see Figure 7-5). *5S Improvement Maps should be hung in a central location with suggestion cards attached so anyone can suggest improvements.*

5S Pocket Manuals

A 5S Pocket Manual can be created that contains five pillar definitions and descriptions, and is small enough to fit into the pocket of work clothes. Shopfloor workers, supervisors, and managers can all use 5S Pocket Manuals for easy reference to the 5S essentials.

5S Department Tours

When one department in a company has implemented the five pillars successfully, it can serve as a model area for other departments to come visit. Since "seeing is believing," this technique is ex-tremely effective for promoting 5S implementation throughout a company.

5S Months

Companies should designate two, three, or four months every year as "5S Months." During these months, various activities such as 5S seminars, field trips, and contests can be carried out to further promote 5S implementation in the company.

TAKE FIVE

Take five minutes to think about this question and to jot down your answer.

- What are some other ideas of how you might promote 5S activities in your workplace? Name at least three.

In Conclusion

SUMMARY

The fifth pillar, Sustain, means to make a habit of properly maintaining correct procedures over time. No matter how well implemented the first four pillars are, the 5S system will not work for long without a commitment to Sustain it.

In your life in general, why do you commit yourself to sustain a particular course of action? Usually you do this because the rewards of keeping to the course of action are greater than the rewards for departing from it. Similarly, if the rewards of implementing the five pillars are greater for you than the rewards of not implementing them, sustaining them through the fifth pillar should be something you take to naturally.

Unlike the first four pillars, the Sustain pillar cannot be implemented by a set of techniques, nor can it be measured. However, you and your company can create conditions or structures that will help Sustain the commitment to 5S implementation.

To Sustain 5S activities in your company, both you and the company management have important roles to play. Part of this role involves creating the conditions that Sustain 5S activities. The other part involves demonstrating that you are committed to Sustain these activities, too. Some of the tools to help Sustain 5S activities in your company include: 5S Slogans, 5S Posters, 5S Photo Exhibits and Storyboards, 5S Newsletters, 5S Pocket Manuals, 5S Department Tours, and 5S Months.

REFLECTIONS

- What did you learn from reading this chapter that stands out as being particularly useful or interesting?

- Do you have any questions about the topics presented in this chapter? If so, what are they?

- What information do you still need to fully understand the ideas presented?

- How can you get this information?

Chapter 8: Reflections and Conclusions

CHAPTER OVERVIEW

Reflecting on What You've Learned

Applying What You've Learned

- Possibilities for Applying What You've Learned
- Your Personal Action Plan

Opportunities for Further Learning

Conclusions

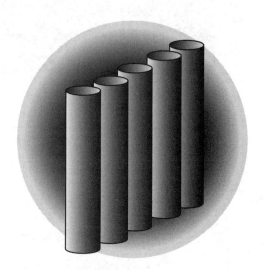

Reflecting on What You've Learned

Key Point

An important part of learning is reflecting on what you've learned. Without this step, learning can't take place effectively. Now that you've come to the end of this book, we'd like to ask you to reflect on what you've learned. We suggest you take ten minutes to write down some quick answers to the following questions.

- In Chapter 1 you considered the question, "What do I want to get out of reading this book?"

    - Have you gotten what you wanted to get out of this book?
    - Why or why not?

- What ideas, tools, and techniques have you learned that will be most useful in your own life, at work, or at home? How will they be useful?

- What ideas, tools, and techniques have you learned that will be least useful in your own life, at work, or at home? Why aren't they useful?

Figure 8-1. Practicing the Outlining Strategy at Home

Applying What You've Learned

Possibilities for Applying What You've Learned

OVER VIEW

The way you decide to apply what you've learned will, of course, depend on your situation. If your company is launching a full-scale 5S implementation program, you should have ample opportunity to apply what you've learned at work. In this case, you may be included on a team of people who are responsible for implementing the five pillars in a certain work area. You may have implementation time structured into your work day and may be responsible for reporting the results of your activities on a regular basis.

Key Point

On the other end of the spectrum, your company may have no immediate plans to implement the five pillars. In this case, the extent to which you can implement what you've learned will depend on how much control you have over your own schedule, work flow, and work area. *However you plan to apply what you've learned about the five pillars, a good place to start practicing 5S concepts and tools is at home.* We have seen people who react to the learning presented in this book by spending an entire weekend applying the five pillars to a basement woodworking area, clothes closet, or garage (see Figure 8-1). This, of course, may have its own limitations, since it's likely that your family has not read this book and may have questions about your 5S activities.

Your Personal Action Plan

Key Point

Whatever your situation, *we suggest you create a personal action plan for how you will begin applying the information you have learned from this book.* You might start by referring to your own notes about the tools and techniques you think will be most useful to you, then writing down answers to the following questions.

- What can I implement right now at work that will make my job easier, better, or more efficient?

- What can I implement at home right now that will make activities there flow more easily or more efficiently?

- How can I involve others at home and at work in the implementation of what I've learned?

When you've answered these questions, we suggest that you commit to completing the things you've written down in a specific period of time and to making a new plan at the end of that time period.

Key Point

It's often good to start with something small that you can comfortably finish in the time you've allowed yourself. If the project is too ambitious or time-consuming you can easily get discouraged and give up.

Key Point

Also, projects you can work on for short periods of time whenever you get a chance are ideal in the beginning. For example, you might decide to reorganize a storage area, one set of shelves at a time, in five- or ten-minute chunks.

Opportunities for Further Learning

Here are some ways to learn more about the five pillars.

- Find other books or videos on this subject. Several of these are listed on the next page.

- If your company is already implementing the five pillars, visit other departments to see how they are using 5S tools and techniques.

- Find out how other companies have implemented the five pillars.

Conclusions

The 5S approach is a simple but powerful method for shopfloor improvement. We hope this book has given you a taste of how this method can be helpful and effective for you in your work. Productivity Press welcomes your stories about how you apply the five pillars in your own workplace.

Further Reading About the 5S System

The following resources available from Productivity Press will provide you with additional education about various aspects of the five pillar system.

Productivity Press Development Team, ed., **5S for Operators Learning Package** (Productivity Press, 1996)—This Learning Package set is designed to help you lead an employee learning group in your company using *5S for Operators* as the reading material. Each package includes the sourcebook *5 Pillars of the Visual Workplace*, a *Leader's Guide*, overheads, slides, and five copies of *5S for Operators*.

Productivity Press Development Team, ed., **5 Pillars of the Visual Workplace** (Productivity Press, 1995)—This is the sourcebook for *5S for Operators*. It includes case studies, numerous illustrations, and detailed information about how to initiate and manage a five pillar implementation effort in any company.

M. Greif, **The Visual Factory: Building Participation Through Shared Information** (Productivity Press, 1991)—This book shows how visual management techniques can provide "just-in-time" information to support teamwork and employee participation on the factory floor.

Nikkan Kogyo Shimbun (ed.), **Visual Control Systems** (Productivity Press, 1995)—This book presents articles and case studies which detail how visual control systems have been implemented in a variety of companies.

H. Hirano, **JIT Factory Revolution: A Pictorial Guide to Factory Design of the Future** (Productivity Press, 1989)—This picture book of JIT includes many before and after photos showing how JIT has actually been implemented in production and assembly plants. Chapter 3 provides an in-depth look at the five pillar system.

Video / Tel-A-Train and the Productivity Development Team
The 5S System: Workplace Organization and Standardization
5S is a method front-line workers can really use to improve workplace safety, reduce waste, simplify work processes, improve equipment maintenance and troubleshooting, and ensure product quality. It's the basis for any on-the-floor improvement activity. Now, using learn-while-doing training techniques, workshop teams can follow this step-by-step video training at their own pace, and implement 5S in their own target area. This complete video training program introduces you to each of the 5S activities and its rationale, and powerfully leads your team through implementation. Includes seven video tapes (90 min. total), facilitator's guide, and participant's guide.

About the Authors

Hiroyuki Hirano

Hiroyuki Hirano was born in Tokyo, Japan in 1946. He graduated from Senshu University's School of Economics in 1970, then joined a large software company to work in the consulting division. There he laid the conceptual groundwork for Japan's first full-fledged production management system. Leaving the software company, he established JIT Management Laboratory Company, Ltd. Using his personal interpretation of the just-in-time philosophy (which emphasizes ideas and techniques for the complete elimination of waste), Mr. Hirano helped bring the JIT production revolution and JIT sales and distribution concepts to dozens of companies in Japan as well as major firms worldwide.

The Productivity Press Development Team

Since 1981, Productivity Press has been finding and publishing the world's best methods for achieving manufacturing excellence. At the core of this effort is a team of dedicated editors and writers who work tirelessly to deliver to our customers the most valuable information available on continuous improvement. Their various backgrounds—art history, English literature, graphic design, instructional design, law, library science, psychology, philosophy, and publishing—provide a breadth of knowledge and interests that informs all their work. Inspiring results is their purpose. They love beautiful books and strive to create designs that please as well as ease our readers' use of our books. They read endlessly to keep abreast of new terminology and changes in both the manufacturing and publishing industries. They learn from our customers' experiences in order to shape our books and off-the-shelf products into effective tools that serve our customers' learning needs.

Melanie Rubin

Instructional Designer Melanie Rubin is a former staff member of the Client Services Division of Productivity, Inc. where she developed training programs for top management and shopfloor teams. Prior to joining Productivity, Ms. Rubin worked for Health Care Coalition, a consulting company offering training in continuous improvement methodologies for hospital systems. Her experience includes development of educational programs for adults in a range of media, including books, standup trainings, and videos. Ms. Rubin received her masters degree in instructional design from the University of Massachusetts, Boston.